THE WORDS WE ALL KNOW . . .

exotic/esoteric *Exotic* means very strange or unusual (*Lions are in danger of becoming exotic even in Kenya.*); *esoteric* means known or understood by only a few (*the esoteric writings of Madam Blavatsky*).

militate/mitigate To *militate* means to fight or have force (*a new campaign to militate against drug abuse*); to *mitigate* means to soothe or make less hostile (*He mitigated her anger by sending flowers.*).

principal/principle A *principal* is the head of a school (*North is the principal of the Hommocks school.*); a *principle* is a moral rule or overarching law (*the accepted principle of doing unto others what you want done to you*).

THE
NEW AMERICAN
DICTIONARY OF
DIFFICULT WORDS

Carol-June Cassidy and **Paul Heacock** are lexicographers. She has worked on the *Cambridge Dictionary of American English* and the *Cambridge Encyclopedia of the English Language*, among other similar titles. Paul Heacock is managing editor of the *Cambridge Dictionary of American English* and was also American English editor of the *Cambridge International Dictionary of English*.

THE
NEW AMERICAN
DICTIONARY
OF
DIFFICULT
WORDS

Carol-June Cassidy
and Paul Heacock

A SIGNET BOOK

SIGNET
Published by New American Library, a division of
Penguin Putnam Inc., 375 Hudson Street,
New York, New York 10014, U.S.A.
Penguin Books Ltd, 27 Wrights Lane,
London W8 5TZ, England
Penguin Books Australia Ltd, Ringwood,
Victoria, Australia
Penguin Books Canada Ltd, 10 Alcorn Avenue,
Toronto, Ontario, Canada M4V 3B2
Penguin Books (N.Z.) Ltd, 182-190 Wairau Road,
Auckland 10, New Zealand

Penguin Books Ltd, Registered Offices:
Harmondsworth, Middlesex, England

First published by Signet, an imprint of New American Library,
a division of Penguin Putnam Inc.

First Printing, January 2001
10 9 8 7 6 5 4 3 2 1

For Tyler, who we hope will one day find it in her heart to forgive us the endless hours of inane word talk during breakfast, lunch, dinner, and all points in between.

Acknowledgments

We wish to thank our editor, Hugh Rawson, for calling this book into being. Without him, the arcane and difficult words we knew before would be gathering cranial dust, and we'd never have discovered all the others we found and included in these pages. We'd also like to thank our agent, Sallie Gouverneur, who offered suggestions that helped us hone the proposal from which this book grew and who obtained for us the big bucks that allowed us to retire to a villa in Nice to write it. We also appreciate the encouragement and advice of the many family members, friends, and acquaintances, logophiles all, who suggested words for inclusion and otherwise urged us on ("Is that book done yet?"), with a special tip of the lexical hat to two Ransoms, Mike and Cory.

We also acknowledge that, while many people helped us with this book, any errors of omission or commission are strictly our own.

Contents

[x] Contents

What Is a Difficult Word?

It is probably easier to agree on what constitutes an easy word than on what constitutes a difficult one. Everyone knows that *cat, girl, table,* and *car* are easy words. There's no question about what they mean, how they're spelled, or—with the possible exception of *girl*—when it's appropriate to use them.

Difficult words are the ones that are troublesome. They are words that people often misuse, words whose meanings are somewhat obscure, words that are regularly confused with other words, and words that are notoriously hard to spell correctly. They are the words you encounter from time to time that seem vaguely familiar but whose meanings remain elusive, the words you half-comprehend from context. They're the words you'd like to use but shy away from using because you aren't entirely sure you are using them correctly. They're the words that would be fun to have at hand when you want to baffle an opponent at Scrabble, dazzle your friends in conversation, or impress your English teacher or colleagues at the office.

The New American Dictionary of Difficult Words includes words that are in use in American English at the dawn of the twenty-first century, words that have been culled from current periodicals and books aimed at well-educated general readers. No attempt has been made to include the most obscure words possible, nor have we tried to incorporate terminology from the more arcane sciences or obsolete items from the early days of modern English. Instead, we have included difficult words that crop up in general contexts and have given clear definitions and realistic examples of their use.

In addition to the words defined and exemplified in the A to Z listing, we have also included a listing of the most commonly misspelled words and, at each alphabetic break in the text, words that are commonly confused with each other. Also included are several sidebars offering information about words dealing with death and dying, with prophecy, with words derived from people's names, and more. At the entries themselves, you will also find notes on the origins of words, their proper usage, and cross-references to similar words or words having the opposite meaning, when appropriate.

We hope this book will prove to be a useful and enjoyable addition to your reference shelf and that it will provide the bon mot for every occasion.

Carol-June Cassidy & Paul Heacock
January 2001

Conventions Used in
the Dictionary

PARTS OF SPEECH

adj.	adjective
adv.	adverb
conj.	conjunction
fig.	figurative examples
n.	noun
phrase	
pl. n.	plural noun
prefix	
v.	verb

CROSS-REFERENCES

Cross-references appear both at entries in the A to Z body of the dictionary and within the Confusables listings. The main body of the dictionary contains cross-references to:

antonyms and synonyms defined in the dictionary

> **supine** . . . Antonym: **prone.**
> **logogram** . . . Synonym: **ideogram.**

related and sometimes confused words

> **creole** . . . Compare **patois; pidgin.**

related words that provide useful information

> **limen** . . . See also **liminal.**

or form part of a set

> **quarto** See also **folio, octavo, quire.**

words in the Confusables lists

> **principal** see at P CONFUSABLES
> **moral** see **ethical/moral** at E CONFUSABLES

and from alternate spellings to the spelling at which the word is defined

> **aeolian** *adj.* see **eolian**

The Confusables contain cross-references from the second or latter element to the place at which an entry is alphabetized

> **happen/transpire** see **transpire/happen** at T CONFUSABLES
> **vulgar/obscene/profane** see **obscene/profane/ vulgar** at O CONFUSABLES

Words—so innocent and powerless as they are, as standing in a dictionary, how potent for good and evil they become in the hands of one who knows how to combine them.

—Nathaniel Hawthorne

Frequently Misspelled Words

Some words can be described as difficult because they are obscure, or of foreign origin, or are used mostly by specialists in particular fields. Then there are the words whose meaning and usage are fairly straightforward, which are known by most reasonably well-educated speakers and writers of English, but which are difficult because it is hard to remember exactly how they should be spelled. The following list shows how to spell the words that are most frequently misspelled.

absence	athletic	clique
accidentally	attendance	coming
accommodate	battalion	committee
accommodation	beginning	comparative
achieve	believe	connoisseur
achievement	believable	conscience
analyze	business	conscientious
apparent	calendar	conscious
argument	category	convenient
assistant	changeable	criticize

definite	height	parallel
definitely	humorous	pastime
delegitimize	immediately	piquant
delegitimatize	incidentally	performance
description	independent	permanent
desirable	independence	perseverance
desperate	indispensable	personnel
disappear	insistent	penicillin
disappearance	irresistible	possess
disappoint	jewelry	possession
dissatisfied	laboratory	precede
eligible	lightning	preferred
embarrass	liqueur	prejudice
embarrassment	losing	privilege
environment	maintenance	procedure
equipped	maneuver	proceed
exaggerate	mathematics	professor
excellent	medieval	pronunciation
excellence	milieu/milieux	pursue
exhilarate	miniature	questionnaire
existence	mischievous	receive
experience	misspell	recommend
familiar	misspelled	repetition
fascinate	necessary	restaurant
foreign	noticeable	rhythm
forty	occasion	rhythmical
gauge	occasionally	ridiculous
government	occurred	sacrilege
grammar	occurring	sacrilegious
grievous	occurrence	schedule
grievance	omitted	seize
harass	omission	separate
harassment	opportunity	separation

similar	tragedy	until
sincerely	transferred	vacuum
succeed	transferring	villain
succession	truly	weird
supersede	tyranny	withhold
surprise	unanimous	writing
technique		

A

CONFUSABLES

abundance/plethora An *abundance* is an ample amount (*an abundance of sunshine*); a *plethora* is an excessive amount (*a plethora of work that needs to be done today*).

accessary/accessory The spelling *accessary* used to refer to people who aid in an illegal activity, and *accessory* was used for additional or subordinate things; now *accessory* is the preferred spelling for either meaning.

adventurous/adventuresome/venturous/venturesome *Adventurous* and *venturesome* are more commonly used to describe people who enjoy adventure (*an adventurous young woman * For a middle-aged guy, he's pretty venturesome.*); *adventuresome* and *venturous* are more commonly used to describe events (*an adventuresome afternoon* * *a venturous vacation in the Andes*).

adverse/averse An *adverse* circumstance is an unfavorable one (*an adverse situation*); if someone is *averse* to something, they are repelled by it or find it distasteful (*She's averse to spending more than she absolutely has to.*).

affect/effect *Affect* is usually used as a verb and means "to influence, persuade, or cause emotion" (*The play affected us deeply.*) or "to pretend to be or have" (*She affected the style of a Hollywood starlet.*), though it can also be used as a noun in psychology to mean "something that arouses the emotions" (*one of the affects that brings on this rage*); *effect* is usually used as a noun meaning "result" (*One of the effects of this drug is sensitivity to light.*), "influence" (*Does eating Twinkies have an effect on your personality?*), or "impression" (*He piles up books and magazines to give an intellectual effect to the place.*), though it can be used as a verb meaning "to cause to be" (*He tried to effect a settlement in the months-old dispute.*); *effects* are "personal belongings" (*Diamonds and emeralds were among her effects when she died.*).

afflatus/flatulence An *afflatus* is an instance of divine inspiration (*What afflatus caused her to paint this masterpiece?*); *flatulence* is the effects or symptoms of digestive gas (*His* *flatulence made him the laughingstock of his classmates.*).

allude/refer To *allude* to something is to refer to it indirectly (*She alluded briefly to "personal problems," but didn't specify what they were.*); to *refer* is to mention directly (*She referred to each of the issues that had been written about in the article.*).

alternate/alternative Both *alternate* and *alternative* are used to indicate additional possibilities (*some alternate destinations*) (*an alternative workout routine*) and can be used as nouns or adjectives; *alternate* can also mean occurring in turn every other time (*alternate Thursdays*).

amoral/immoral An *amoral* act is one that displays no regard for right or wrong (*The pursuit of profit can be viewed as being completely amoral.*); if something is *immoral* it is intrinsically wrong (*The bombing of civilian targets was clearly immoral, and possibly criminal.*).

amuse/bemuse see **bemuse/amuse** at B CON-FUSABLES

anxious/eager If someone is *anxious* they are upset, unhappy, or uncomfortable about a situation (*anxious to please*); someone who is *eager* can hardly wait (*eager to get started*).

apprehend/comprehend To *apprehend* something is to see that it exists (*They toured the war-torn country to apprehend the damage that was done*) or have a deep, basic understanding of it (*It's hard to truly apprehend the criminal mind*); to *comprehend* something is to grasp its full meaning (*It's hard for laypeople to comprehend quantum mechanics.*).

assay/essay As verbs, *assay* means to test or analyze (*The police lab will assay the substance.*); *essay* means to try (*He was loath to essay some of the more exotic foods being proffered by his host.*).

aught/naught *Aught* can mean either "all" (*She tried again and again, but aught was in vain.*) or "nothing, zero" (*a score of twelve-aught*); *naught* means "nothing, zero" (*Their efforts came to naught.*). The sense of *aught* meaning "nothing" came from a miswriting of *a naught* as *an aught*.

authentic/genuine see **genuine/authentic** at G Confusables

avert/avoid To *avert* something is to stop it from happening or to turn away (*avert your eyes * avert a catastrophe*); to *avoid* something is to stay away from it (*Have you been avoiding me lately?*).

abase *v.* to make lower in standing, position, or social status: *I wouldn't abase myself with such contemptible activities.*

abasement *n.* *the abasement suffered by those who made their condition publicly known should be an embarrassment to us all.*

abashed *adj.* somewhat embarrassed and disconcerted or self-conscious: *The kudos offered during the award ceremony left her exhilarated and slightly abashed.*

aberrant *adj.* abnormal or unusual; deviant: *Epidemiologists and climatologists believe the aberrant virus outbreak is due to unusual weather conditions favoring the survival of greater numbers of the mice that carry the disease.* ∗ *Everyone is concerned by his aberrant behavior.*

aberration *n.* a deviation from what is normal or usual: *This working extra hours of late is an aberration; normally we don't have such difficult deadlines.* ∗ *This version of the proposal seems to contain several aberrations.*

abeyance *n.* a temporary stop or suspension in an activity: *The great moments in one's life are often accompanied by a sense of emotion held in abeyance.*

abhor *v.* to detest something, or to find something repugnant: *I abhor these gray, characterless townhome communities being built just off every major highway.*

abhorrent *adj.* disgusting, detestable, or repugnant: *The attempt to single out the least popular boy and hold him solely responsible was abhorrent.*

ablution *n.* a washing of the hands or body: *Are you done with your morning ablutions yet?*

abnegate *v.* to renounce or relinquish something to which one had been entitled: *By selling his share to his sister, he abnegated any right his children may have had to the family home.*
  abnegation *n. the vows taken by the monks include abnegation of worldly possessions.*

abrogate *v.* to end, especially by formal means: *The company abrogated many of their contracts during the retrenchment.*

abstemious *adj.* consuming food and drink in moderation or sparingly: *He would be less prone to erratic behavior if he would only pursue a more abstemious life, yet he cannot bring himself to do so.*

abstruse *adj.* difficult to understand: *I don't know why, but I find the concept of the international dateline to be totally abstruse.*

abundance see at A CONFUSABLES

abysm *n.* an extremely deep place, or an extreme depth; an abyss: *Her nightmares were filled with empty mazes and endless abysms.*

abysmal   *adj.* **1** extremely bad *This music is abysmal.* **2** limitless or unrelieved *She was lost in an abysmal sorrow.*

abyss   *n.* an extremely deep and sometimes wide place: *a dark abyss*
  abyssal   *adj.* extreme, or immeasurable: *Near the rim of the great abyss of the Grand Canyon, we set up our telescopes to look deeper into the abyssal expanse of the night sky.*

accessary/accessory   see at A CONFUSABLES

accrete   *v.* to grow or make bigger by adding: *Testimony dragged on for weeks, slowly accreting detail until the case was impossibly complex.*

acedia   *n.* sloth; laziness, especially in religious observance: *When I stopped attending Sunday services in my teens because I found it pointless, my mother attributed it to acedia.*

acerbic   *adj.* harsh or bitter: *His resignation letter was laced with sarcastic asides and acerbic remarks.*

acme   *n.* the highest point; the most perfect stage of development: *Her room looked like the acme of luxury.*

acolyte   *n.* **1** a follower or devoted assistant: *Truth can be harmed by an overzealous acolyte.* **2** a person who assists the minister or celebrant in a religious service: *Several acolytes led the procession.*

acrimonious *adj.* bitter or caustic: *While there may be good reason to be upset, these acrimonious comments are out of place here and now.*
  acrimony *n. It was a verbal attack of unexpected acrimony.*

actuarial *adj.* based on statistics and probabilities, especially relating to a person's likelihood of illness or death: *In the actuarial course of events, a man can expect to predecease his wife while escaping breast cancer.*

adamantine *adj.* of an inflexible or unyielding nature: *The defense presents an adamantine logic that follows from the basic premise. ∗ I admire his strong will and adamantine perseverance.*

adduce *v.* to suggest, or cite as evidence: *New trends in popular literature have been much adduced by critics and social commentators.*

à deux *adj.* involving only two people, usually romantically: *Would a conversation and perhaps a drink à deux be in the cards?*
  à deux *adv. I was hoping we might be able to dine à deux this evening.*

adjudicate *v.* to settle judiciously; to judge: *New York City's former mayor could be found regularly adjudicating on* The People's Court.

adjunct *n.* an additional but less important part of something: *They were chided for acting as if the*

U.K. were some sort of adjunct to U.S. foreign policy objectives in Europe.

admonish *v.* to warn or scold someone, or to remind someone of a responsibility: *I have to admonish my daughter to eat a decent lunch.*
   admonishment *n.* a reminder, warning, or reproof: *a gentle admonishment*
   admonition *n.* an act of admonishing: *The admonition came from the principal.*

adulate *v.* to praise or flatter excessively: *The film was not much watched or adulated when it appeared, but it was looked back on as evidence of how a great director developed his techniques.*

adumbrate *v.* to intimate or give evidence of a future possibility: *It seems clear that he did not intend to include this story in the original manuscript, and was considering possibilities adumbrated elsewhere in the text.* * *All the bizarre varieties of sadomasochistic sexuality were lovingly adumbrated in Mapplethorpe's photographs.*

adventurous/adventuresome see at A CONFUSABLES

adverse see at A CONFUSABLES

aegis, egis *n.* sponsorship or patronage: *Under the aegis of the consortium, more students have been sent abroad to study, and member institutions are hosting a growing number of students from other countries.*

aeolian   *adj.* see **eolian**

aesthete, esthete   *n.* a person with refined taste and a love of the arts: *Marion is an aesthete, and her move into writing art criticism should work well for her.*

aesthetics   *n.* **1** beauty as a physical aspect or quality of something: *I thought it pointless to debate the aesthetics of strip malls.* **2** the philosophical study of the nature of beauty, especially in regard to the fine arts: *a theory of aesthetics*

affable   *adj.* pleasant, friendly, kind, and easy to get along with: *He was stiff and obviously uncomfortable, and his attempts at being affable were a complete failure.*
   affability   *n.* friendliness and kindness: *She has an air of affability about her that makes you want to go over to her and strike up a conversation.*

affect   see at A Confusables

affinity   *n.* **1** a feeling of connection with something, of suitability to do something, or of similarity to something: *He carried a long, fearsome-looking shotgun that had a marked affinity to a cartoon weapon.* **2** a feeling of strong mutual attraction: *I felt a powerful affinity toward her, and she felt the same toward me.*

Artistic Temperament

A few fancy words are used to define people who display either a strong appreciation for the arts or a complete lack of interest there.

aesthete, esthete *n.* a person with refined taste and a love of the arts.

aesthetics *n.* **1** beauty as a physical aspect or quality of something **2** the philosophical study of the nature of beauty, especially in regard to the fine arts.

dilettante *n.* **1** someone with an interest in but only superficial experience or knowledge of art **2** a lover of the arts.

litterateur *n.* a writer or a person devoted to studying literature.

philistine *n.* someone who is without intellectual or cultural interests, or who is indifferent or hostile to art and culture.
    philistine *adj.* lacking intellectual or artistic interests.
    philistinism *n.* indifference to anything cultural or intellectual.

afflatus *n.* an inspiration or brilliant impulse: *There are those who truly enjoy public speaking,* *while others cherish their afflatus but are more happily engaged sweating over blank sheets of paper.* See also A CONFUSABLES.

afoot *adj.* beginning to happen or in progress: *Changes are afoot in the commercial world.*

aggregation *n.* a collection, group, or pile of various things: *The attic holds an aggregation of what was once desirable but now molders unused and forgotten.*

Agonistes *n.* someone who is both an actor and a combatant or struggler (used after the name of the person who fills this role): *With this short speech before a roomful of former Cold Warriors, Nixon Agonistes had triumphed yet again.*

agrostology *n.* the scientific study of grasses: *Chase was the principal scientist for agrostology at the Institute.*

alacrity *n.* cheerful readiness or willingness: *The photographer circulated among the guests with alacrity, finding a good mix of candid and formal shots.*

albeit *conj.* although, even though, or notwithstanding: *It was a clear and sunny, albeit hot, day.*

alchemy *n.* a seeming magical ability to cause transmutation, or a medieval form of chemistry concerned especially with attempts to change base metals into gold: *The script was weak and the play seemed doomed, but the director has worked some kind of alchemy.*

alchemical *adj. Computer engineering is an alchemical enterprise that hasn't quite achieved gold.*

algolagnia *n.* sexual pleasure that is obtained by giving or receiving pain: *This dominatrix was a queen of algolagnia—she gave pleasure by causing pain and got pleasure from inflicting it.*

algorism *n.* the decimal system: *Computation in algorism is not a universal approach to numbers.*

alliterate *v.* to repeat a sound in two or more words in a group, such as the same first or last letters of several words in a line of poetry: *The words alliterate in most of the rhymes and songs the children learn in preschool.*
    alliterating *adj. The alliterating strains of Peter Piper wafted down the hallway.*
    alliterative *adj. She overuses the alliterative device in such statements as, "The punctilious perfectionism of the players' performances provide a paucity of provocation."*

allogeneic, allogenic *adj.* having genetic differences while being of the same species: *Patients who need new bone marrow must often resort to allogeneic transplants from donors.*

allude *v.* to refer to indirectly or casually: *Alluding to the last merger of six years ago, many employees said they felt they had been sold out for the second time.* See also A CONFUSABLES.

alluvial *adj.* made up of sediment deposited by moving water: *During the diamond rush, the alluvial surface of this gravel wasteland was shoveled up and put through screens.*

alternate/alternative see at A CONFUSABLES

amalgam *n.* a combination of different things: *The far-flung Roman empire was an amalgam of peoples and traditions.*
    amalgamate *v.* to combine different things to-gether: *The Smithsonian amalgamated the Center for African American History and Culture with the Anacosta Museum in 1995.*
    amalgamation *n.* the result of combining or mixing different things together: *The final script was an amalgamation based on myths, fables, and fairy tales.*

amanuensis *n.* an assistant or secretary; someone who takes dictation: *She had the ability to lead one on and draw out one's train of thought, an ability so essential in an amanuensis.*

ambience, ambiance *n.* the particular qualities of an environment that make it unique: *The place has some wonderful beers, but the ambience—striving young men in suits, heavy cigar smoke, and far too much noise—leaves a lot to be desired.*

ambient *adj.* surrounding; enveloping: *There was a degree of ambient crispness in the kitchen at that hour of the morning.*

ambivalence *n.* conflicting feelings or an attitude toward someone or something that is neither completely positive nor negative: *Her ambivalence about signing with us led us to withdraw the contract.*

> **ambivalent** *adj.* having neither completely positive nor completely negative feelings about something, or without a clear preference for one thing over another; uncertain: *You can pick a restaurant—I'm ambivalent this evening.*

ambulatory *adj.* **1** able to walk, and not confined to bed or a wheelchair: *After two months in a cast, it will take a little while to become fully ambulatory again.* **2** movable or moving from place to place: *Our ambulatory party went from bar to bar, stopping in and then moving to the next place.*

ameliorate *v.* to make something better, to become better, or to improve: *High blood pressure can often be ameliorated with weight loss and exercise.* * *to ameliorate a problem*

> **ameliorative** *adj. The problem of classroom overcrowding has been discussed many times, but no ameliorative measures have yet been taken.*
> **amelioration** *n. Blair quickly introduced several ameliorations to Thatcherism.*

amity *n.* friendship; peace and understanding: *Marriage between royal families was political, a pledge of amity between two nations.*

amoral see at A CONFUSABLES

amorphous *adj.* having no definite shape or form: *These artisans create amorphous things that may be fun and decorative, but can not be called art works.* ∗ *To many of his colleagues, he was an amorphous character, hardly noticeable among his peers.*

amplitude *n.* fullness, magnitude, or largeness in scope, breadth, or range: *The amplitude of the welcome was overwhelming.* ∗ *The judges were impressed in equal measure by her poise, presentation, and the tone, quality, and amplitude of her voice.*

amuse see **bemuse/amuse** at B CONFUSABLES

anachronistic *adj.* out of the proper order or time; of an earlier time or state: *His musical repertoire is painfully anachronistic, and that's why he can't find work.*

anagram *n.* a word or phrase made from the reordered letters of another word or phrase, or a game in which words are made from a group of randomly picked letters: *"Satin" is an anagram of "stain."*
    anagrammatically *adj.* by rearranging the letters of a word or the words of a sentence: *The puzzle is solved anagrammatically.*

analogous *adj.* similar to or corresponding in some way to something else: *The belief that bigger, faster computers will one day learn to think is a fallacy analogous to reasoning that if humans run fast enough they will fly.*

analysand   *n.* someone who is being psychoanalyzed: *When Gerry explained that he's a psychologist and wanted to ask about the macabre Halloween decorations, the willing analysand readily agreed.*

anapest   *n.* in poetry, a metrical foot consisting of two short or unstressed syllables followed by a single long or stressed syllable: *Unable to speak, dogs can nonetheless produce a passable anapest if you encourage them to speak: "Woof woof woof."*

anastomosis   *n., pl.* **anastomoses** the interconnection of parts of a system that form it into a network, such as blood vessels or the branches of a river: *We are led to believe that the framework holding together the strands of the argument will be understood, but in the end the book fails to make clear this anastomosis.*

anathema   *n.* **1** someone or something damned or cursed, or a curse or excommunication: *The priest was excommunicated and declared anathema.* * *An anathema by the Roman Catholic Church on the work of Galileo was not fully nullified until centuries after his death.* **2** something shunned or disliked intensely: *Avant-garde music is anathema to this group of classical devotees.*

    anathematize   *v.* to pronounce an anathema upon; to curse or denounce: *To anathematize an entire generation because of the excesses of a minority is simply unfair!*

    anathematization   *n. You should have expected that presenting such an irreverent view of Ameri-*

*can nationalism in your film would lead to boy-
cotts and anathematization.*

anfractuous   *adj.* full of twists and turns; winding
or circuitous: *It was a perilous journey along an
anfractuous mountain road that was often little more
than a path.* *   *The anfractuous route took me
through Atlanta, Dallas, and Detroit on my way
from New York to Seattle.*
　anfractuosity   *n.* the state of being twisting and
turning, or a course or way of thinking that is
anything but direct: *The anfractuosity of his discourse led some students to think he was a genius,
while others reacted by taking long naps in his
classes.*

angels   *n.* the lowest of nine orders of angels
　angel   *n.* a member of the lowest angelic order,
or a member of any of the nine orders of the
celestial hierarchy.

The Celestial Hierarchy

To most people, an angel is an angel, and if it's
a really cute angel, you might call it a cherub.
Traditionally, however, there are nine levels of
celestial beings. Ranked from the lowest to the
highest, they are angels, archangels, principalities, powers, virtues, dominions, thrones, cherubim, and seraphim.

---

anima   *n.* the soul or life force: *The paintings seem to leap to life with an anima bestowed by the painter.*

> In Jungian psychology, anima is the inner personality, or the female principle present in a man.

animus   *n.* strong dislike or ill will; animosity: *My animus against this type of violent action movie was not shared by my friends.*

annelid   *n.* a segmented worm: *He kept earthworms, leeches, all manner of squiggly annelids.*
annelidous, annelid, annelidan *adj.* of or having to do with an annelid or worm: *The mud in many places was churned up by numbers of some kind of annelidous animal.*

annulus   *n.* a ringlike structure or mark, such as a growth ring on a fish's scales or a group of cells found on some ferns: *A small annulus is visible toward the center of the CD.*

anodyne   *n.* something that relieves pain or distress: *The doctor prescribed an anodyne that included codeine.* * *Your smiling face was just the anodyne I needed.*
anodyne *adj. Judy finally relaxed under the anodyne influence of the music.*

anomaly   *n.* an action or thing that is unusual, abnormal, or not of the regular type or method: *Small anomalies in the texture of our daily routine led me to suspect something had gone terribly wrong.*

anomalous *adj.* unusual; abnormal: *These anomalous weather conditions are being attributed to the Pacific current known as El Niño.*

anomie, anomy *n.* the collapse of or lack of social norms and values, or alienation and purposelessness: *The anomie and disconnectedness that afflict the characters in this novel seem a little too pat.* * *We tired of his complaints, his despair, his anomie—if his life was pointless, there wasn't much point in hearing about it.*

anoxic *adj.* having a very low amount of oxygen: *Lower New York Bay was severely anoxic, but it has begun to recover.*

antepenult, antepenultimate *n.* the third syllable from the end of a word: *He rhymes on the antepenult, matching "oscillating" and "fossil."*
antepenultimate *adj.* relating to the third from the end: *the antepenultimate phrase.* Compare **penultimate**.

antinomianism *n.* the belief of some Christians that salvation depends only on faith, independent of morality: *To justify vigilantism by claiming the law doesn't adequately punish criminals is a modernist antinomianism that ignores the vigilante's own criminal, immoral behavior.*
antinomian *n.* a person who believes this doctrine

antipathy *n.* an instinctive aversion to or natural dislike for something: *Sean has always been a vege-*

tarian; his antipathy for meat was clear before he turned two.

antiphon   *n.* a verse chanted or sung in two alternating parts, usually a statement and response, especially as part of religious worship: *When the antiphon is sung, the congregation will give the response.*

    antiphonal   *adj.* chanted or sung in two parts by alternating voices: *A lot of rap music is antiphonal in structure.*

    antiphony   *n.* alternating response; speech or song that is responsive in structure: *I enjoy the antiphony of the playwright's dialogue.*

antipodes   *n.* a place that is on the other side of the earth from where you are: *As she traveled those antipodes, she was overcome by a sense of longing for home.*

    antipodean   *adj.* being directly opposite or on the other side of the earth: *They hiked those antipodean mountains more than once.*

anxious see at A CONFUSABLES

aperçu   *n., pl.* **aperçus** an outline or sketch of an initial impression: *After a whirlwind tour of the region, he was asked to prepare an aperçu that could serve as the basis for preliminary discussions.*

aphaeresis, apheresis   *n., pl.* **aphaereses, aphereses** the loss of letters or sounds at the beginning of a word, resulting in a new, shorter word: *Through* *aphaeresis, "anatomy" came to be construed as "an atomy" in the sixteenth century.*

aphelion *n.* the point on the orbit of a planet or other celestial body that is farthest from the sun: *Earth will reach its aphelion on July 3.*

apheresis *n.* see **aphaeresis**.

aphorism *n.* a wise or clever saying: *His best-known remark is probably the aphorism "Tell me what you eat and I'll tell you who you are."* Compare **apothegm**.

apocalypse *n.* **1** devastation and doom: *The apocalypse of nuclear destruction was unleashed on Japan.* **2 the apocalypse** the end of the world.
   apocalyptic *adj. After the earthquake, the city lay in apocalyptic ruin.* * *an apocalyptic vision*

> Apocalypse is a name given to any of the works in a genre of post-Biblical Jewish and early Christian religious writings that are claimed to be divine revelation and often foretell the end of the world, in particular, the Book of Revelations in the New Testament.

apocrypha *pl. n.* writings of questionable authorship or authenticity: *Whole books are written on the apocrypha sometimes attributed to Shakespeare.*
   apocryphal *adj.* false or of doubtful origin: *an apocryphal tale*
   (see note next page)

The Apocrypha is a group of fourteen books that were included in the Old Testament in very early versions of the Greek and Latin Bibles and are not considered canonical by Protestants. Apocrypha also refers to early Christian writings that were rejected as part of the New Testament and not part of the Catholic or Protestant canons.

apoplectic *adj.* experiencing an intense emotion, especially of annoyance, anger, or rage: *The executive director was apoplectic when a report on the confidential merger negotiations appeared in the morning paper.*

apostate *n.* someone who has abandoned their religion, faith, cause, party, etc.: *An apostate, he continued to work among the poor, but no longer as a missionary, having left the mission, priesthood, and church.*
   apostate *adj. Whether Christian, agnostic, pagan, or apostate—My what a day this promises to be!—they'll all be home for Christmas.*
   apostasy *n.* the abandonment of one's faith, cause, party, etc. *The secretary's apostasy is well known—he didn't just leave the administration, he disavowed its policies and principles.*

apothegm *n.* a short and concise remark, saying, or aphorism: *Mike, as usual, neatly summed up the situation with a pithy apothegm.* Compare **aphorism**.

apotheosis *n.* a glorified ideal, a person or thing that is glorified, or something that represents the highest level of achievement for its type: *This style of cooking reached its apotheosis in English public schools, and I wanted nothing to do with it.*

apparition *n.* a ghost or other mysterious creature that appears suddenly and surprisingly: *He rounded the bend and there she was, an apparition in flowing white, seemingly floating at the side of the road.* Compare **revenant**.

   apparitional *adj.* ghostlike: *There is something apparitional in the moment, and it chills and excites them.*

apprehend see at A CONFUSABLES

approbation *n.* approval: *The proposals were met with unanimous approbation.*

apse, apsis *n.* a vaulted, semicircular part of a building, especially a church: *Flouting convention, he made the room dome-shaped, like the apse of a cathedral.*

arcana *pl. n.* details and information that are obscure or exotic and known only to a few: *Charlie's eighty-year-old mom is very knowledgeable about baseball arcana.* The singular form, **arcanum**, is rarely used.

   arcane *adj.* obscure and understood by few people: *The arcane procedures of the copy department ensure a high-quality product.*

archaic   *adj.* from an earlier time; antiquated: *A review will be carried out to revise the archaic rules governing transfer of ownership.*
  archaism   *n. The archaism of the process causes unnecessary delays.*

archangels   *n.* the second of nine orders of angels.
  archangel *n.* an angel of the order of archangels; a chief angel
  See THE CELESTIAL HIERARCHY at **angel**

archetype   *n.* based on or copied from the original one of its type: *The archetypal nineteenth-century lighthouse at Cape Hatteras was in danger of being inundated by the ocean.* Related adj.: **prototypical**.

architectonic   *adj.* architectural, or having a design or structure that appears to be architectural: *He uses flying buttresses to give a medieval motif to his architectonic designs.*

ardent   *adj.* with or showing passion or enthusiasm: *We met for the first time with this small, ardent group of scholars.* Synonym: **fervent**.

arras   *n.* a fancy tapestry or wall-hanging: *She was hiding behind the tattered arras, planning to jump out when he came past.*

arriviste   *n.* someone whose success, wealth, or power was only recently gained; an upstart: *She's an arriviste who built a technology empire in three* *years on her own innovative ideas and a few strategic acquisitions.* Compare **parvenu.**

artifact, artefact *n.* a product or result, especially something characteristic of an age or culture: *This is a specialty cable station broadcasting shows that are artifacts of the 1960s.* * *Viking artifacts*

ascetic *n.* a person who believes material things are unimportant and who lives simply, especially someone who devotes his or her life to prayer and contemplation: *Kirk may be a philosopher and he may shun computers even for his writing, but he is no ascetic.*

    asceticism *n.* simplicity and austerity, usually in material things, or severity: *Harry is a rather flamboyant personality, so the asceticism of his house was surprising.*

ascribe *v.* to attribute or regard as belonging to; to assign or credit: *English writers in the Middle Ages would ascribe authorship of their works to God.*

asperse *v.* **1** to attack by spreading false or malicious statements: *You would asperse your own mother if you thought it would get you elected.* **2** to sprinkle with holy water: *Babies are aspersed at baptism.*

aspirational *adj.* having as a goal, desire, or ambition; of something to which one aspires: *This cottage is my aspirational country retreat.*

assay see at A Confusables

assiduous *adj.* careful or persistent and attentive in attending to details: *With assiduous planning and exacting execution, they might just be able to carry out the heist.* ∗ *We were easily able to find the information we needed thanks to the research staff's assiduous record-keeping.*

  assiduously *adv. I worked assiduously day and night to finish the book, but it was still overdue when I handed it in.*

assuage *v.* to calm, relieve, or lessen something felt or experienced: *Environmental issues can raise ethical questions, and it was often necessary to assuage some moral insecurity raised during the question-and-answer session.*

asymmetrical, asymmetric *adj.* lacking similarity in the placement of elements to either side of a central line; lacking balance: *The garden is set on a simple rectangular plot that is made more interesting by an asymmetrical layout.* Antonym: **symmetrical**.

atavistic *adj.* **1** reflecting an earlier style or way of life, or suggestive of something primitive: *I felt an atavistic yearning to have my mother comfort me.* ∗ *The sport of boxing has been attacked as violent and atavistic.* **2** having the characteristics of a remote ancestor: *an atavistic trait*

  atavism *n.* **1** a throwback or reversion to an earlier condition or way of being: *One would hope* *that young people would reject a 70s atavism, especially once they appraised the repugnant fashions of the time.* **2** a characteristic of a remote ancestor: *Looks like his must be the expression of some ancient atavism.*

atlantes *pl. n.* see **atlas**.

atlas *n., pl.* **atlantes, atlases** a supporting column sculpted in the form of a male figure: *At the back of the house, overlooking the river, is a portico, its roof held by eight atlantes.* Synonym: **telamon**. Compare **caryatid**.

atomy *n.* a tiny particle or a very small creature: *His research delves into the worlds of atomies.*

Atomy originally meant a skeleton, or a very skinny person, and derived from the mistaken spelling of *anatomy* as *an atomy*.

atrabilious, atrabiliar *adj.* **1** inclined to a melancholy attitude: *Given her atrabilious character, she had expected rejection.* **2** having a peevish disposition: *He is known in the field as one of the most atrabilious historians and seems happiest when he is venting his spleen.*

atrophy *v.* to waste away or cause to deteriorate from disuse: *Over the years, my carpentry skills had atrophied.*

attaint   *v.* to disgrace or to stigmatize: *The Constitution's protection of a citizen's right to protest does not prevent other citizens, or even law enforcement or governmental bodies, from attainting the effort.* ∗ *Not a hint of scandal attainted the family name.*

attenuate   *v.* to make something thin, short, diluted, or weak: *The drone of the radio attenuated his ability to concentrate on his work.*
   attenuated   *adj.* weakened, shortened, or diluted: *She complained loudly about her students' attenuated attention spans.*
   attenuation   *n.* something that lessens, weakens, or dilutes: *He's learned to be patient with her repetitions and attenuations.*

Augean   *adj.* filthy, degrading, or corrupt: *Tabloid TV indulges in Augean exposés and out-and-out lies.*

> In classical mythology, the stables of King Augeas, containing three thousand cattle, had not been cleaned in thirty years when at last they were washed by the river Alpheus, diverted there by Hercules.

aught see at A CONFUSABLES

augur   *v.* to predict; point to: *The deal augurs a new era of corporate ownership.*
   augury   *n.* **1** the ability to make predictions: *You were right about the change in the market—I'm impressed with your augury.* **2** a sign or omen: *So*

far the auguries point to a successful third quarter.
Compare **divination**; **omen**; **portent**; **prognostication**.

auriferous *adj.* containing gold: *Erosion revealed the veins in the auriferous outcrop.*

auspicious *adj.* favorable; indicating success: *The rain had stopped and the sky was clear—it was an auspicious start to the day.*

austere *adj.* having a severe and uncompromising attitude or appearance: *Andrea's work has an austere coolness that distinguishes her from her contemporaries.*
　　austerity *n. I'm used to warm colors and a bit of clutter around me, so I feel unnerved by the austerity of these rooms.*

auteur *n.* a film director whose movies are personal and unique: *Why would auteurs subject themselves to the indignities of Hollywood filmmaking?*

authentic see **genuine/authentic** at G CONFUSABLES

autodidact *n.* someone who is self-taught: *She's an autodidact, and frankly, she's reading the works of the classical dramatists in the original Greek just for the fun of it.*

autologous *adj.* taken from the individual who receives it: *Patients can bank their own blood and later receive autologous blood transfusions.*

autonomous   *adj.* not subject to outside control; independent: *The futuristic vision of autonomous robot-run industry has never really come to pass.*

avaricious   *adj.* greedy: *Tweed's political machine was a coalition of Irish immigrant working-class interests and avaricious bluebloods.*

avatar   *n.* the embodiment of something, or a personification: *Clinton is, in many ways, the avatar of his era, as presidents sometimes prove to be.* ∗ *Once thought to be the avatar of Woodstock Nation, he later embraced capitalism with equal enthusiasm.*

In Hinduism, an avatar is the incarnation of a deity. Hindu literature relates several incarnations of the Hindu deity Vishnu, most notably as the avatar Krishna in the Bhagavad-Gita, and as each of the three Ramas in the Ramayana.

averse   see **adverse/averse** at A Confusables

avert   see at A Confusables

avidity   *n.* eagerness, dedication, or enthusiasm: *I've never understood your avidity for cooking—I find the process tiresome, though I enjoy the outcome.*

avoid   see **avert/avoid** at A Confusables

avuncular   *adj.* friendly and benevolent in a manner thought to be typical of a kindly uncle; like an uncle: *Gerry likes to challenge the kids in his teasingly avuncular way.*

B

CONFUSABLES

baroque/rococo Both words describe ornate, elaborate art, architecture, music, or literature, but *baroque* works tend to be grotesque and contrasting (*baroque, bombastic organ music*), while *rococo* works incorporate elaborate designs to produce a fine, delicate effect (*the rococo filigree on a carved wooden screen*).

basal/basic Both words mean essential or fundamental, but *basal* describes things that are necessary for maintaining life (*the basal organs, such as the heart*) and things used to instruct beginners (*basal texts*); *basic* means characteristic of a chemical base (*a basic reaction*) or containing little silica (*a basic stratum*) as well as the more general sense of fundamental (*a basic mistake*).

bathos/pathos A theatrical or literary work that displays *bathos* shows characteristics such as triteness, sentimentality, or insincerity (*Identification with the characters that was built in the first act is destroyed by the bathos of the second.*); similar works displaying *pathos* show sadness, sympathy, or pity (*the pathos evoked by an orphaned infant*).

bemuse/amuse *Bemuse* means to confuse or bewilder (*I was bemused by her insistence on calling me her brother*); *amuse* means to entertain humorously or enjoyably (*I was not amused by her constant references to my baldness.*).

benign/malign *Benign* means harmless (*a benign tumor*), or having a gentle disposition (*a benign, caring individual*); *malign* means harmful and becoming worse (*a malign tumor*), or evil in nature (*a malign personality*).

benefactor/beneficiary A *benefactor* provides benefits (*The organization's benefactors contributed to the fund.*); a *beneficiary* receives benefits (*the beneficiary of a rich uncle's gifts*).

bereaved/bereft Both words can mean suffering from the death of a loved one (*She was inconsolably bereaved when her son died.*); *bereft* can also mean lacking something (*He is completely bereft of common sense.*).

bizarre/macabre see **macabre/bizarre** at M CONFUSABLES

blatant/flagrant *Blatant* acts are crass, offensive, and vulgar (*He shows a blatant disregard for his neighbors.*); *flagrant* acts are purposefully immoral or illegal (*a flagrant breach of the treaty*).

bloc/block A *bloc* is a group of people, countries, or organizations joined to achieve a common purpose (*the Democratic bloc in the state assembly*); a *block* is a solid piece of material (*a butcher's block * toy blocks*) or a rectangular shape formed by intersecting city streets (*walk around the block*).

bountiful/fulsome see **fulsome/bountiful** at F CONFUSABLES

browse/peruse *Browse* means to read casually (*I browsed a few magazines as I stood there.*); *peruse* means to study attentively (*Carefully peruse the text to see if you can find the errors.*).

---

bain-marie *n., pl.* **bains-marie** a large pan holding hot water in which smaller pans are placed to cook food slowly or to keep their contents warm: *Baking in a bain-marie requires no oven.*

ballyhoo *v.* to advertise in an enthusiastic way: *In Cape Town, ballyhooed as a great vacation spot, tourism is booming.*

banal *adj.* common and dull; of a boring and uninteresting type: *Press speculation about Clinton's sexual peccadillos during his first presidential campaign were banal in comparison to the feeding frenzy unleashed by the Lewinsky affair.*

    banality *n. I could do without the banality of another "friendly" get-together with the senior staff.*

baroque see at B CONFUSABLES

basal see at B CONFUSABLES

basic see **basal/basic** at B CONFUSABLES

bathos see at B CONFUSABLES

bathypelagic *adj.* having to do with or living in the ocean depths between 2,000 and 12,000 feet (600 and 3,600 meters): *bathypelagic fishes.* Compare **pelagic**.

beatific *adj.* blissful, happy, or saintly: *Natasha's face has the empty, beatific intelligence of some of Matisse's supine women.*

bedizen *v.* to decorate or adorn, especially gaudily: *She was bedizened in a black leather outfit that clung so closely it left little to the imagination.*

behoove *v.* to be necessary, correct, or appropriate for: *It does not behoove us to throw away* *that which is useful when we discard what we do not want.*

belie   *v.* to contradict or misrepresent: *The amount of noise they made belied their small number.*

bellicose   *adj.*   hostile;   aggressive;   belligerent: *Something must have happened to bring on this bellicose mood; you don't just wake up that nasty.* Synonyms: **pugnacious; truculent**.

bemuse   *v.* to confuse or bewilder someone, or to be confused or bewildered: *We were bemused by the sudden, unexplained change of plans.* See at B CONFUSABLES
  bemused   *adj. Ann gave me a bemused look, and I realized she hadn't gotten the message I left on her machine earlier.*
  bemusement   *n. Francine had no idea what Mike was talking about, and her bemusement was obvious to everyone but him.*

benefaction   *n.* the act of providing help, especially by donating money, or a contribution of money: *The benefactions of wealthy alumni supported the university's construction program.*

benefactor see at B CONFUSABLES

beneficiary see **benefactor/beneficiary** at B CONFUSABLES

benevolent   *adj.* kind and showing goodwill: *In this picture you feel a sense of communion between the* *benevolent elderly man and the sleeping child at whom he gazes.*

benign   *adj.* **1** kind, gentle, or favorable: *a benign experience* **2** not harmful: *a benign tumor* See at B CONFUSABLES

benthos   *n.* creatures living at the bottom of a sea or a lake, or the bottom of a sea or lake itself: *The British Royal Navy used a weighted line to sound the benthos between Norway and Iceland in its early explorations.*

bereaved see at B CONFUSABLES

bereft see **bereaved/bereft** at B CONFUSABLES

bespoke   *adj.* made to order; custom-made: *Michael would prefer to have one bespoke shirt from that little tailor in Jermyn Street in London than to have a closetful of off-the-rack Christian Diors.*

bête noire   *n., pl.* **bêtes noires** someone or something that is particularly disliked: *Lillian Hellman is Melnick's and Levin's most heinous bête noire.*

betoken   *v.* to be or give as a token, sign, or evidence of something: *Mom said when the wind blew in from the direction of the water it betokened a coming storm.* ∗ *Matt can't be here today, but the flowers he sent betoken his good wishes.*

bibliolatry *n.* **1** excessive belief in a literal interpretation of the Bible: *The bibliolatry of his co-workers made Charlie a little nervous at first.* **2** excessive devotion to books: *Erin had been a bibliophile, but developed into a fanatic, besotted by bibliolatry.*

bifurcate *v.* to divide into two branches: *Rocks and sediment buildup out in the middle of the water bifurcated the original flow, creating these two streams.*
  bifurcation *n. I didn't remember seeing this bifurcation of the trail on the map I'd consulted before we set off.* Compare **dichotomy**.

bildungsroman, Bildungsroman *n.* a novel about the moral and psychological growth of its main character: *The plot is a typical bildungsroman about a young man choosing art over everything else.*

birl *v.* to spin, or to cause a floating log to spin with your feet: *He birled the rollers with the heel of his hand.*

bizarre see **macabre/bizarre** at M CONFUSABLES

blatant/flagrant see at B CONFUSABLES

blithe *adj.* cheerful, carefree; showing no sign of cares or worries: *He sat in his office, blithe and happy, talking about his plans for the coming year.*

bloc/block see at B CONFUSABLES

boiserie *n.* wood paneling for the walls of a room, especially carved wood paneling: *I especially liked the stone fireplace and boiserie in the study.*

bolus *n.* a soft, rounded mass or lump: *Dropping a neat bolus of mashed potatoes on plate after plate, I realized two things: I hate working in a catering kitchen, and I'll never have a reception at one of these wedding factories—never, never, never.*

bombastic *adj.* pretentious and overblown in speech or writing; important sounding: *That bombastic fogy finds something to go on about at every meeting. * It was another bombastic campaign-trail harangue.*

bonhomie *n.* a friendly, good-natured manner: *Harry's a great tour guide—he brings energy, encyclopedic knowledge, and a natural bonhomie to the job.*

boondoggle *v.* to deceive or try to fool someone: *Her charade was unnecessary to begin with, and now she's boondoggled herself into a very embarrassing position.*
    boondoggle *n.* a pointless endeavor; something done that is of no value: *The program wasn't just a failure, it was a complete boondoggle.*

bosky *adj.* **1** having lots of trees, bushes, or shrubs: *The bosky hills behind the house are full of game birds.* **2** of or relating to a forest or woods: *These bosky predators will do more damage than all the clear-cutting loggers combined.*

bounden   *adj.* obligatory or binding: *Journalists consider it their bounden duty to probe the personal lives of anyone who decides to run for public office.*

bountiful see **fulsome/bountiful** at F CONFUSABLES

bowdlerize   *v.* to modify something, usually something written, by changing or removing parts because someone finds those parts objectionable; to expurgate: *The perfectly manicured garden struck me as false—a bowdlerized version of nature.*

braggadocio   *n.* pretentious boasting and bragging, or a person who brags: *His self-aggrandizing braggadocio was by turns tedious and infuriating.*

breve   *n. esp. British* a double whole note.

breviary   *n.* a book of daily prayers: *It wasn't that obvious that he's a minister, but his breviary gave him away.*

brindled   *adj.* having a gray or yellowish brown color with darker stripes or spots: *Ann hasn't chosen the drapes yet, but she's considering something brindled and a lighter weight fabric. * You'll easily recognize the tawny, brindled feral dogs on the island—if they let you see them, that is.*

brio   *n.* animation and vivacity: *You have to be impressed by his dash and brio, his freewheeling virtuosity and optimism.*

Keeping Time in British Music

British English uses an entirely different set of words to describe the lengths of notes. The mysteries of these terms are hard for a speaker of American English to fathom. The longest notes are based on a double whole note, while a whole note is referred to as half of that unit. And the longest word describes the shortest note.

breve *n.* a double whole note.

semibreve *n.* a whole note.

minim *n.* a half note.

crotchet *n.* a quarter note.

quaver *n.* an eighth note.

semiquaver *n.* a sixteenth note.

demisemiquaver *n.* a thirty-second note.

hemidemisemiquaver *n.* a sixty-fourth note.

Brobdingnagian *adj.* gigantic, enormous, or tremendous: *My debt has grown to Brobdingnagian proportions.* See BOOK WORDS 2.
(see note next page)

> In *Gulliver's Travels* by Jonathan Swift, Brob-
> dingnag is a land where everything is gigantic.

brood   *v.* to constantly think about or worry over
something: *You've been brooding about that argument for weeks now—get over it.* Compare **muse**.

brooding   *adj.* having a threatening look or atmosphere, especially because of shadows or dim light:
*The narrow, brooding path through the old gardens
brought us suddenly to a sunlit field, where we
stopped to rest.*

browse see at B CONFUSABLES

bruit   *v.* to repeat or spread news or rumors: *It's
being bruited about that the coach's contract won't
be renewed next season.* Bruit is most often used in
the passive and followed by *about*.

bulimarexia   *n.* an eating disorder in which one alternately craves and is disgusted by food; bulimia ner-
vosa: *As a teenager she underwent therapy for
bulimarexia.*

burgeon   *v.* to rapidly develop, grow, or expand:
There is burgeoning interest in swing dance. * *The
U.S. economy has burgeoned throughout the
nineties.*

burnish *v.* to polish, smooth, or brighten: *The burnishing effects of care distinguished even the common objects in the room.*

C

CONFUSABLES

callous/callus *Callous* with an *o* is the verb meaning to thicken skin (*This work will callous your hands.*) and the adjective meaning thick-skinned in its literal and figurative senses (*Some thought Reagan was a callous old man.*); *callus* without an *o* is the noun form (*Calluses formed on her fingers.*).

canvas/canvass The one-*s* *canvas* is the cloth (*paintings done on canvas*); the two-*s* *canvass* is both the noun and verb dealing with soliciting votes, opinions, etc. (*to canvass a neighborhood* * *to conduct a canvass of registered voters*).

capital/capitol A *capital* is the city in which a government meets (*Albany is the capital of New York State.*), the accumulated wealth of a person (*He spent his life amassing capital.*), an uppercase letter (*Write all in capitals.*), and the top of a column (*Note the designs on the capitals.*); when used as an adjective, *capital* means punishable by death (*a capital crime*), excellent (*a capital suggestion*), or very serious (*a capital mistake*); the U.S. *Capitol* is the building in which Congress meets, and a *capitol* in any of the states is the building in which the legislature meets.

carat/karat/caret A *carat* is a unit of measurement of the weight of precious stones (*a 40-carat ruby*); a *karat* (also spelled *carat*) is a unit of measurement of the fineness of gold (*a 24-karat gold ring*); a *caret* is the wedgelike symbol (^) used by proofreaders to mark an insertion.

careen/career *Careen* means to tip to one side and is used of vessels at sea (*We careened across the waves.*); it is also used synonymously with *career* to mean to rush headlong in an out-of-control manner (*With no brakes and nothing to impede its progress, our car picked up speed, careering down the steep incline.*).

carrel/carol A *carrel* is a study nook in a library (*Students filled the carrels and slouched in the aisles.*); a *carol* is a Christmas song.

catholic/Catholic The lowercase version is an adjective meaning liberal or universal (*She has* *very catholic tastes when it comes to men.*); the uppercase *Catholic*, both a noun and adjective, refers to the Roman Catholic Church or its members (*Is she a lapsed Catholic?*).

cel/cell A *cel* is a transparent piece of plastic or celluloid used in making animated films (*He bought an original cel from* Who Framed Roger Rabbit?); all other senses are covered by the spelling *cell*, including the basic structures of life (*Cells have nuclei.*), a single-room dwelling (*Put her in a cell and throw away the key.*), a basic unit of organization (*a Communist-party cell*), and an atmospheric unit (*a storm cell*).

childish/childlike *Childish* is used to rebuke someone for acting immaturely (*Stop being so childish.*); *childlike* expresses admiration for innocence and trust comparable to that of a child (*a childlike joy*).

chord/cord A *chord* is three or more musical notes sounded together (*three-chord rock music*), an emotional response (*It struck a chord with me.*), a straight line intersecting two points on a curve (*Measure the length of the chord.*), the outside members of a bridge truss, and the length from the leading edge to the trailing edge of an airfoil; a *cord* (also spelled *chord*) is a stringlike anatomical structure (*vocal cords*); a *cord* is also a rope, an electrical wire, a rib on a piece of cloth, a common feeling (*the cord that binds us*), or a stack of firewood.

cite/site To *cite* a source for something is to identify where it came from (*He cited a biblical passage in his defense*); a *site* is a particular place (*a building site*).

common/mutual see **mutual/common** at M CONFUSABLES

complement/compliment A *complement* is a completing part or counterpart (*This wine is a perfect complement to chicken.*); a *compliment* is a flattering remark (*I'll take that as a compliment.*).

comprehend/apprehend see **apprehend/comprehend** at A CONFUSABLES

comprehensive/comprehensible If something is *comprehensive* it is inclusive (*comprehensive insurance*); if someone is *comprehensive* they are capable of readily understanding (*She's comprehensive of foreign languages.*); if something is *comprehensible* it can be understood (*Those mathematical theorems are not comprehensible to me.*).

comprise/compose *Comprise* means to include and is used to describe a whole (*The team comprises veterans and rookies.*); *compose* means to make up and describes the parts (*Veterans and rookies compose the team.*).

connote/denote *Connote* means to imply (*Does his silence connote agreement?*); denote means to designate or announce (*A yellow light denotes caution.*).

contemptible/contemptuous *Contemptible* means worthy of disdain and is used to describe others (*You're a contemptible lout!*); *contemptuous* means expressing contempt or disdain (*She gave me a contemptuous sneer and walked away.*).

continual/continuous *Continual* means uninterrupted forever (*the sun's continual production of heat and light*); *continuous* means not stopping from beginning to end (*the longest continuous run in Broadway history*).

council/counsel A *council* is a group of people serving as a legislative, executive, or advisory body (*The council met in closed session.*); a *counsel* is a lawyer (*Will counsel for the defense please approach the bench?*); *counsel* can also be advice (*You should seek counsel from a qualified practitioner.*).

curse/epithet see **epithet/curse** at E CONFUSABLES

cabal *n.* a conspiratorial group; people who devise a plot or intrigue: *Nomination of school board candidates is controlled by a cabal from the city's wealthiest neighborhoods.*

cabala, cabbala, cabbalah *n.* see **kabala**

cadence *n.* a rhythmic pattern, beat, or flow: *She fell asleep to the lulling cadence of her dad's song.*

caitiff *n.* a despicable coward: *What sort of caitiff would attack a man's character without making himself known?*
    caitiff *adj.* despicable; cowardly: *Such caitiff behavior is deplorable.*

cajole *v.* to urge or persuade someone to do something using flattery or soothing words: *He woos and cajoles her, hoping she will approve.*

Cajun *n.* a person descended from French settlers expelled from Canada in the late eighteenth century who settled in Louisiana and Maine, or the French dialect spoken by Cajuns. Compare **Creole**.

calcar *n., pl.* **calcaria** a spur or projection, especially the projection at the base of a flower petal or on the wing or leg of a bird: *Bats use the calcar as a sort of thumb with which they can climb trees.*

callous see at C CONFUSABLES

callow   *adj.* young and inexperienced, or immature: *Now the heads of major corporations, they started out as callow entrepreneurs who built these computer and electronics businesses from the ground up.*

callus see **callous/callus** at C CONFUSABLES

calumny   *n.* a false and malicious statement intended to damage someone's reputation: *If you intend to seek public office, prepare yourself to face a nearly endless stream of calumny and abuse.*
  calumniate   *v. My intention was never to impugn or calumniate, I was merely describing things as I saw them.*

canard   *n.* a misleading or untrue story or rumor: *While there may be more jobs for accountants than for concert pianists, the claim there are no careers in music is just a canard.*

candescence   *n.* glowing white heat: *Although the flames had died down, the logs' candescence kept us cozy long into the night.*

canonical, **canonic**   *adj.* pertaining to that which is authorized, recognized, or officially sanctioned, especially ecclesiastical law, liturgy, or sacred books: *Some works that are canonical in the Roman Catholic church are part of the Protestant Apocrypha.* See **Apocrypha**.

cantle *n.* a piece, usually a corner: *This is my office—a cantle, a piece of turf that is mine alone.* ∗ *Snorkeling near the coral reefs, we had up-close views of a cantle of the watery world we'd never seen before.*

canvas/canvass see at C CONFUSABLES

capacious *adj.* roomy; spacious: *The house looked small from the outside, but the rooms were sunlit and capacious.*

capital/capitol see at C CONFUSABLES

caprice *n.* a whim or fancy that leads to an action: *His childhood had been ruled by a bewildering combination of caprice and control.*
　　capricious *adj. This guy is a capricious and difficult client.* ∗ *I didn't know Walter had this capricious side.*

carapace *n.* a hard covering or shell, especially on an animal: *On its way through the Bronx, the train travels beneath a carapace of highway crossovers and bridges connecting one end of a street to the other.* ∗ *a turtle with a brown-black carapace*

carat/caret see at C CONFUSABLES

careen/career see at C CONFUSABLES

caricatural *adj.* like a caricature; having or made to have exaggerated elements: *There is nothing par-*

ticularly caricatural about Nast's early drawings for Leslie's Illustrated Newspaper.

carol see **carrel/carol** at C CONFUSABLES

Carolingian   *adj.* pertaining to the time of Charlemagne's rule: *a Carolingian book of hours* ∗ *the Carolingian empire*

carrel see at C CONFUSABLES

cartouche   *n.* **1** an ornamental frame: *The painting is unadorned by fancy cartouche or plain steel rim* **2** an oval surrounding a king's or queen's name, especially on ancient Egyptian monuments

caryatid   *n., pl.* **caryatids, caryatides** a supporting column sculpted in the form of a draped female figure: *The raised fountain in the garden is supported by a caryatid.* Compare **atlas**; **telamon**.

castigate   *v.* to punish or severely criticize: *Parent groups castigated the school district for spending millions of dollars on work that has nothing to do with education.* Compare **chasten, chastise**.
  castigation   *n. I was anxious to avoid further castigation.*

catafalque   *n.* the platform or structure on which a body lies in state: *Citizens waited in line for hours to have their brief moment before the catafalque.*

catholic/Catholic see at C CONFUSABLES

cavalcade *n.* a procession or series: *Few Americans could name the entire cavalcade of presidents.*

cel see at C CONFUSABLES

celerity *n.* swift motion or rapid action: *The virus, carried by droplets of saliva, spreads with celerity to anyone coming within yards of an infected patient.*

cell see **cel/cell** at C CONFUSABLES

cellarer *n.* a person, especially in a monastery, who is responsible for maintaining the supply of provisions: *If we are indeed out of victuals, the cellarer will certainly be called to account.*

censorious *adj.* critical, condemning, or reprimanding: *I tried to see myself through my mother-in-law's censorious eyes and realized she would never approve of me.*
    censoriously *adv. The Senator departed from his prepared speech and commented censoriously on Congressional wrangling over the funding bill.*

cerulean *adj.* of a deep blue color: *The crystalline cerulean sky that accompanies daybreak never fails to lift the spirits.*

cerumen *n.* the yellowish, waxlike substance that lines the ear canal; earwax: *Before testing your hearing, the audiologist will want to remove any excess cerumen.*

chaconne   *n.* a slow, stately dance thought to be of Spanish origin, or music played in ¾ time for this dance: *The evening's dancing ended with a chaconne.*

chanson   *n.* a song, usually one sung in French, especially a cabaret song: *Jeanne's half-hour of entertaining chansons was the high point of the party.*

charnel   *n.* a building or place where bodies or bones are put.
  charnel   *adj. There were charnel deposits near the building, leading investigators to suspect it had been used as an execution site.*

chary   *adj.* cautious or watchful: *Most of the northeastern states have become chary about the effect of development on natural resources.* Synonym: **wary**.

chasten   *v.* to correct or improve by punishing: *I was chastened by my teacher and admonished to pay more attention next time.* Compare **chastise, castigate**.

chastise   *v.* to punish or reprimand publicly, especially officially or in print: *Editorialists across the country chastised the president for his decision.* Compare **chasten, castigate**.

chef-d'oeuvre, *n., pl.* **chefs-d'oeuvre** an artistic or literary masterpiece: *Few scholarly monographs would be considered a chef-d'oeuvre.*

cherubim *n.* the eighth of nine orders of angels
  cherub *n., pl.* **cherubs**, **cherubim** an angel of the second highest order. See THE CELESTIAL HIERARCHY at **angel**.

chiaroscuro *n.* the light and shade in a picture or drawing: *The chiaroscuro of these drawings strikes me as foreboding, and at odds with the subject matter.*

chiasmus *n.* a reversal of the order of words in two phrases that are otherwise identical or parallel: *She took Mae West's famous chiasmus—"It's better to be looked over than to be overlooked"—as her motto.*

chicanery *n.* deceit and trickery: *The chicanery involved, while deplorable, did not amount to an actual crime.*

childish/childlike see at C CONFUSABLES

chimera *n.* something imagined; a fanciful notion: *Disgruntled scholars would be better off writing critiques rather than plumping for the chimera of so-called inclusion.*
  chimerical *adj. Yeats's vision of a life with Maud Gonne, his one true love, proved chimerical.*

In classical mythology, a Chimera is a fire-breathing monster, usually represented as having the head of a lion, the body of a goat, and the tail of a dragon.

chord see at C CONFUSABLES

choucroute *n.* a bouffant hairdo; big hair: *She was amazed to see that here in the hinterlands, women still wore a choucroute without apparent embarrassment.*

cicerone *n., pl.* **cicerones, ciceroni** a guide, especially for sightseers: *If you are looking for a literary tour of New York's Greenwich Village, you'll find Harry the ideal cicerone.*

Cimmerian *adj.* extremely dark or gloomy: *She composes Cimmerian verse of an unutterably depressing nature.*
   Cimmerian *n.* a creature that lives in total darkness: *Some of these sea creatures are genuine Cimmerians, and the concern is that explorers' lights may be blinding them.*

> In classical mythology, the Cimmerian people inhabit a remote land described by Homer as a place of perpetual mist and darkness.

cincture *n.* a belt or girdle, especially a sash worn by nuns or priests: *Sister Edgar wore the old things with arcane names, the wimple and the cincture and the guimpe.*

cinerary *adj.* of or for the ashes of the dead: *The funeral director showed us the cinerary urns available in that price range.*

cipher *n.* **1** someone without strong characteristics or qualities; a nonentity: *He's someone who makes no impression, a cipher, but that's a disguise he works hard to perfect.* **2** a code: *notes written in a cipher* **3** a zero: *A one followed by too many ciphers—that's what it cost!*

circadian *adj.* relating to twenty-four-hour biological rhythms: *Open throughout the afternoon, the tulip bud closes at dusk, following a circadian pattern tuned to the sun.*
  circadian rhythm *n.* a daily, 24-hour activity cycle: *Working nights had disrupted Steve's circadian rhythm and caused him to become depressed.*

circumambient *adj.* surrounding on all sides: *The circumambient odors were repugnant, choking his senses.*

circumlocution *n.* evasive speech or the use of great numbers of complicated words to express a relatively simple idea: *The circumlocutions of these self-important academics serve only to highlight their tremendous feelings of inadequacy and insecurity.*

circumnavigate *v.* to travel completely around the circumference of something, especially the earth, or to travel around rather than through an area: *Unfortunately, while you may not want to visit the* *museum's largest and most popular room, there is no way to circumnavigate it.*

circumscribe *v.* **1** to limit the range of something: *A lack of funds can certainly circumscribe your vacation options.* **2** to draw a line around something: *A low cordon circumscribes the edge of Stonehenge beyond which visitors are not permitted.*
    circumscribed *adj. She had had way too much to drink, and could only walk taking tiny, circumscribed steps, picking her way home haltingly.*

cite see at C CONFUSABLES

clement *adj.* mild, pleasant, or temperate: *On Sunday mornings, in clement weather, they bring lawn chairs and the Sunday paper to the park by the water.*

cloture *n.* a parliamentary method of ending debate and bringing a matter to an immediate vote: *Under the Senate's rule for cloture, as few as forty-one Senators can keep a measure from being voted on.*

coalesce *v.* to come together into a uniform whole: *Race, sex, and revolution coalesced in the person of Eldridge Cleaver, an attractive, charismatic black man who promised to overthrow the establishment.*

codex *n., pl.* **codices** an ancient manuscript comprised of a number of pages, usually a quire, folded or sewn together; a manuscript volume of an ancient text: *Funding for the exhibition of the Leonardo codex was supplied by its owner, Bill Gates.*

codicil   *n.* an addition as a supplement or appendix to a legal document, especially one made to a will: *When our daughter became disabled, we added a codicil to our will establishing a trust for her.*

coeval   *n.* equal in age or length of existence: *Merryl was her coeval, a girl who had many of the same experiences.*

cogent   *adj.* reasoned, convincing, or to the point: *The speaker's delivery was lucid and cogent.* * *a cogent argument*

cognate   *adj.* **1** related by blood; having a common ancestor, especially on the mother's side: *The law forbids marriages between cognate relatives.* **2** related in function or analogous in nature or character: *After learning how an air pump works, the cognate functions of a water pump should be readily understood.* **3** related in origin to other words in related languages that have developed from the same root: *In most Germanic languages, the various words for fire are all cognate, sharing a common ancestor.*
  cognate   *n.* **1** someone related by blood to another: *My mother's genealogical research has uncovered cognates dating back to the 1500s.* **2** a word in one language that is related to one in

another language: *The German word* Feuer *and the English word* fire *are cognates.*

cohort *n.* **1** a group, especially one of people who have something particular in common: *He arrived without his usual cohort—only his family was with him.* **2** a supporter, associate, or companion: *Andrew and two of his cohorts were responsible for all of the planning.*

coign see **quoin**.

colloquial *adj.* conversational, or appropriate to everyday speech and writing: *When campaigning, she addresses her constituents with a friendly, colloquial informality.*

colluvium *n., pl.* **colluviums, colluvia** loose soil of sand, pebbles, and rock that collects especially on the lower parts of a slope: *The trail here was steep, and the dry colluvium made the footing difficult and sometimes dangerous.*

columbarium *n., pl.* **columbaria** a building or burial vault with recessed spaces to hold the cremated ashes of the dead: *Don's ashes weren't left in a columbarium, but sprinkled into the Pacific as he'd wanted.*

comestible *adj.* suitable for eating; edible: *The company has diversified into comestible products such as soft drinks, while maintaining its presence in the health-care market.*

comestible   *n.* something that can be eaten: *Carter's eponymous comestible, Billy Beer, had a short shelf life in supermarkets but has since become a valuable collectible.*

Food Words

The culinary world offers up a feast of interesting words. These are but a few of the terms describing food, methods of cooking, people involved in obtaining and eating food, and words about meals. Dig in!

bain-marie   *n., pl.* **bains-marie** a large pan holding hot water in which smaller pans are placed to cook food slowly or to keep their contents warm.

cellarer   *n.* a person, especially in a monastery, who is responsible for maintaining the supply of provisions.

comestible   *adj.* suitable for eating; edible; or *n.* something that can be eaten.

commensal   *n.* a dining companion.

decoct   *v.* to extract flavor from something by boiling, or to concentrate or reduce by boiling.

esculent   *adj.* edible; usable as food.
  esculence   *n.* the quality of being edible or of being worth eating.

---

piquant *adj.* having a pleasingly sharp, tangy flavor; tart.

pith *n.* the fibrous, white matter under the peel of a citrus fruit.

postprandial *adj.* occurring after a meal.

prandial *adj.* having to do with a meal.

commensal *n.* a dining companion: *I arrived late and my commensals were already seated.*

commensurable *adj.* comparable by the same measure or standard; proportionate: *The vendor has changed packaging, but the new containers are commensurable with what we were getting before.* Antonym: **incommensurable**.

commensurate *adj.* of equal amount, size, or degree to something else: *Their lifestyle is commensurate with their income.* Antonym: **incommensurate**.

common see **mutual/common** at M CONFUSABLES

compeer *n.* **1** someone of equal rank; a peer: *While some widows of public officials become respected public figures in their own right, she withdrew from the public, leading a quieter life than her compeers.* **2** a companion or associate: *Tonino introduced his compeer as "Wife," although she surely had a name.*

complement see at C CONFUSABLES

complicit *adj.* involved as a partner or accomplice: *My husband was complicit in keeping me from finding out about the surprise party.*
    complicity *n.* involvement with someone, especially in some wrongdoing: *The husband of a board member was accused of complicity with the roofing contractor in rigging the bid.*

compliment see **complement/compliment** at C CONFUSABLES

compose see **comprise/compose** at C CONFUSABLES

comprehend see **apprehend/comprehend** at A CONFUSABLES

comprehensible see **comprehensive/comprehensible** at C CONFUSABLES

comprise see at C CONFUSABLES

concatenation *n.* an interlinked series: *It was a curious concatenation of aspirations and inadvertencies that got me to Harvard.*

concupiscence *n.* sexual desire or longing; lust: *Andrea had a bit of a reputation for her concupiscence, for which we loved her and forgave her.*
    concupiscent *adj. Ah, summer in the city—the heat, the smog, the concupiscent catcalls of the construction crews.*

condescend   *v.* to behave in a way that implies one is of a higher social or moral position; to do something in a patronizing or haughty way: *He finally condescended to talk to me.* * *I offer to help and they start yelling at me for condescending.*

　　condescending   *adj.* patronizing: *a condescending smile*

congruent   *adj.* **1** corresponding or in agreement or harmony; congruous: *He believes that, despite remaining differences, the lives of men and women are more likely to be congruous today than at any time in history.* **2** coinciding exactly when placed one atop the other: *congruent triangles*

conjecture   *v.* to reach a conclusion or form an opinion based on very little or unreliable evidence: *I don't know how it works, but I would conjecture that this little valve lets in some sort of fuel.* Compare **divine**.

　　conjecture   *n. His refusal to declare his candidacy leaves him open to all sorts of conjecture and speculation.*

connote see at C CONFUSABLES

consilient   *n.* being in accord or agreement: *the jury heard the consilient testimony of three witnesses this afternoon.*

conspectus, conspectuses   *n.* a general view, survey, or summary: *Any conspectus of the past century must take into account both war and technology.*

consummate *adj.* **1** complete, perfect in every way, or the most skillful or experienced: *She was a consummate role model and loved working with her young protégés.* * *a consummate politician* **2** being the best or most perfect example of something; superb: *Not even Trump, the consummate deal-maker, could obtain the property.*

consummate *v.* **1** to complete or finish something: *We have a letter of intent, and Thursday we meet to sign the contracts, pay the lawyers, and consummate the deal.* **2** to have sex with your spouse for the first time after being married: *He says they never consummated the marriage, so they should be able to get an annulment.*

contemptible/contemptuous see at C CONFUSABLES

contention *n.* controversy or dispute: *No one expected the changes to the cafeteria would cause so much contention.*
    contentious *adj.* quarrelsome, causing conflict or argument, or having a tendency to argue or dispute: *Discussions over schedule changes became unexpectedly contentious.* * *Sean just has a contentious nature.*

contiguity *n.* a continuous connection; a state in which separate things touch or follow closely: *She yearned to be closely entwined, yet feel solitude's friendly presence, as warm and undesolating as contiguity itself.*

continual/continuous see at C CONFUSABLES

contumacy *n.* willful stubbornness: *We cannot countenance this sort of contumacy in subordinates.*
  contumacious *adj.* stubbornly willful, rebellious, or disobedient: *Trapped at home with a contumacious toddler for weeks on end, she began to feel inadequate in almost everything she was doing.*
  contumaciously *adv. He contumaciously refused to participate in any of the group activities.*

contumely *n.* mean, harsh, or cruel language that displays contempt or feelings of superiority toward others: *Those in attendance could not believe the contumely heaped upon him by his so-called best friend.*
  contumelious *adj. You don't expect contumelious remarks to be included in a funeral oration.*

conundrum *n.* a riddle or puzzle: *His art presents the moral conundrums faced by victims of violence.*

copacetic *adj.* OK; completely fine: *Although the situation may not be 100 percent copacetic now, everything will be fine in the long run.*

copious *adj.* large in amount or quantity; plentiful; abundant: *The book offers copious details about the diet of the different social classes in France at the time of the revolution.*

coppice *n.* a thicket or grove of trees or shrubs, especially one maintained by periodic cutting or

pruning to encourage the growth of shoots or root
suckers: *Soldiers hunkered down in the coppice,
waiting for their enemies to come into range.*

coprolite   *n.* fossilized excrement: *Back in the lab-
oratory, tests revealed that their find was a coprolite.*

coquette   *n.* a woman whose appeal is purely sexual: *She was just some coquette I'd met at a party,
not someone I'd bring home to meet the family.*
  coquettish   *adj. He asked what she was drinking,
  and she responded with a coquettish smile.*
  coquettishly   *adv. She coquettishly plucks the
  cigarette from his mouth, places it in the ashtray,
  then plants her mouth where the cigarette had
  been.*

cord see **chord/cord** at C CONFUSABLES

cordon sanitaire   *n., pl.* **cordons sanitaires** a line,
demarcation, or barrier around an area established
to quarantine or to prevent entry: *Most New York-
ers are unhappy about the mayor's cordon sanitaire
around City Hall.*

cornice   *n.* a decorative, horizontal molding, usually at the top of a building: *The buildings, with
their identical stoops, windows, and cornices, face
each other, mirror images on either side of the narrow street.*

corollary   *n.* a consequence or result; the thing that
happens because something else happened or ex-

ists: *A rough corollary is that you will get double the computational power for the same price at two-year intervals.*

corporeal   *adj.* physical, bodily, or material: *A visit to the doctor may give evidence of corporeal vigor, or breakdown.*

corpulent   *adj.* large and stout; fat: *A corpulent gentleman of middle age, he always seems somewhat rumpled and bemused.*

coruscate   *v.* to sparkle, or to give off flashes of light: *The crystal goblets coruscated in the candlelight.*
   coruscation   *n. The little ones were taken with the coruscation of the fireworks but didn't like the noise at all.*

cosmology   *n.* 1 a philosophical theory or system of belief explaining the nature of the universe and the place of the individual: *The* Tao *is both a cosmology in itself and a component of a larger Chinese cosmology born of Confucianism.* 2 the study of the structure and development of the universe; a branch of astrophysics: *a course in cosmology*
   cosmologist   *n. She's a cosmologist working at MIT.*

costive   *adj.* 1 causing or suffering from constipation: *The costive effects of such a diet have been well documented.* 2 lacking generosity; stingy: *There*

*was something costive about John—he didn't want
to give anything away.*

coterie   *n.* a close group of people who share an
interest or are someone's followers; a clique: *Marjorie is at a party this evening with her bicycling
coterie.* * *Saddam's security forces are said to be
an extraordinarily loyal coterie who are obedient to
a fault.*

council see at C CONFUSABLES

counsel see **council/counsel** at C CONFUSABLES

coup de théâtre   *n., pl.* **coups de théâtre** a surprising turn of events, or a dramatic or sensational happening: *It was a coup de théâtre unequaled in
American political history.*

crapulous   *adj.* showing signs of eating or drinking
to great excess, or suffering from doing so: *Crapulous Jack lurched to his feet, all rosy and afloat from
the booze.*

credulous   *adj.* **1** inclined to readily believe or be
convinced: *I was joking, but he didn't realize it—I
forget how credulous he is.* **2** readily believed or
believable: *credulous reports*
   credulity   *n.* willingness to believe: *The excuse
   she gave tested his credulity.*

crenellated, crenelated   *adj.* (of battlements and
castle walls) having regular, usually rectangular

spaces along the top: *They stood in the shadow of the crenellated wall.*

creole   *n.* a native language that originated in the combining of two or more distinct other languages: *Papiamento, the language of Curaçao, is a creole based on Portuguese and Spanish.* ∗ *Haitian Creole* Compare **patois; pidgin**.

> **Creole**   *n.* a West Indian or South American of European descent, or a person from the southern U.S. descended from the original Spanish, or in Louisiana the original French settlers; the French-based language spoken by Louisiana Creoles. Compare **Cajun**.

crepuscular   *adj.* dim; like twilight: *We followed the path through the cool, crepuscular shadows of the garden.*

criminate   *v.* to incriminate someone or make someone appear guilty of a crime or fault: *She was tortured in the hope that she might criminate others.*

crotchet   *n. esp. British* a quarter note

cryptoamnesia   *n.* the belief that one has personally thought of or found out about something that was actually heard or learned from someone else: *We've come to accept Grandpa's cryptoamnesia, though it can be irritating.*

ctenophore   *n.* a gelatinous sea creature; a comb-jelly: *Harmless ctenophores washed around our* *ankles where we waded into the sound.* ∗ *The speci-men is a ctenophore that lives in eastern estuaries.*

cultus   *n., pl.* **cultuses, culti** a cult: *The bloody sac-rifices of the cultus seemed like a false expression of piety to him.*

cum   *conj.* and also: *Oliver started working at the magazine as an editor cum book reviewer.*

curse see **epithet/curse** at E CONFUSABLES

cynosure   *n.* someone or something attracting at-tention: *He was flustered to find himself the cyno-sure of everyone in the room.*

D

CONFUSABLES

definite/definitive Something that is *definite* is unambiguous and certain (*I've asked her several times, but she won't give me a definite answer.*); something *definitive* is absolute or final (*a definitive solution*), or the ideal example of something (*Many consider it to be the definitive road car.*).

delegation/legation See **legation/delegation** at L CONFUSABLES

denote/connote See **connote/denote** at C CONFUSABLES

detached/unattached See **unattached/detached** at U CONFUSABLES

diagnosis/prognosis A *diagnosis* is a medical examination, or the opinion derived from such an exam (*My diagnosis is that the cause is just nerves, not anything organic.*); a *prognosis* is a prediction of the probable course of a disease or condition (*The prognosis for a lovesick woman is not good.*).

discrete/discreet A *discrete* entity is separate and distinct (*The discrete parts are then assembled*); a *discreet* entity is one that is modest and respectful of propriety (*She's always discreet, and doesn't talk about others behind their backs.*).

disinterested/uninterested *Disinterested* is usually taken to mean unbiased (*a disinterested judge*); *uninterested* means indifferent or not interested (*I'm uninterested in rock concerts.*), a sense that has also been expressed by *disinterested* since the fifteenth century, although it is sometimes considered incorrect today.

dissemble/disassemble To *dissemble* is to hide the true nature of something (*dissemble amusement behind a stern countenance*), or to simulate (*dissemble the actions of a drunk*); to *disassemble* is to take apart (*After disassembling the bicycle, I couldn't get it back together again.*).

distinct/distinctive *Distinct* can mean separate (*a distinct piece of machinery*), clear (*a distinct sign of approval*), or unlike (*a nose distinct from the others'*); *distinctive* means unique or distinguishing (*His car has a distinctive stripe.*) or characteristic (*a distinctive walk*).

diurnal/nocturnal *Diurnal* means happening every day (*a diurnal job*) or active during the day (*a diurnal creature*); *nocturnal* means occurring nightly (*nocturnal news programs*) or active at night (*nocturnal creatures*).

dribble/drivel A *dribble* is a small trickle, especially of saliva (*I mopped a dribble from baby Sarah's mouth*); a tiny amount of something (*a few dribbles of information*); and the act of bouncing a basketball. *Drivel* can also be a small trickle of saliva but is usually used to mean nonsense (*You expect me to believe drivel like that?*).

dyeing/dying *Dyeing* with an *e* is the act of coloring cloth with dye; *dying* is the cessation of life.

---

dactyl *n.* a metrical foot in a poem which has one long syllable and two short ones or one stressed syllable and two unstressed ones

daedal *adj.* **1** skilled and complicated in design or function; intricate: *The daedal programming required to keep an air traffic control system functioning cannot be created overnight.* **2** skillfully made or used; artistic: *Her daedal handling of these materials shows a superior sensibility.*

de rigueur *adj.* proper, customary, or expected in the circumstances: *Gruesome violence became de rigueur in action films, as car chases had been a generation earlier.*

debacle *n.* a failure, collapse, or rout: *The Willie Horton issue came to symbolize the debacle of the Dukakis presidential campaign.*

decerebrate *v.* to remove the cerebrum, or to stop cerebral brain function: *They engaged in experiments that involved decerebrating cats.*
  decerebrate *adj.* **1** having no cerebral function: *The accident left him decerebrate.* **2** having little intelligence or reason: *What sort of decerebrate fool would suggest attacking the White House?*

declension *n.* **1** a move away from the original or standard of something; a deviation: *What you might call "personalizing" or "making improvements" to the program amounts to a declension from the ideal user environment as designed by the programing team.* **2** the inflected forms of a word considered as a group, or the recitation of the inflected forms of a word: *Sitting in Latin class, my mind went blank and I couldn't remember the declensions of any of the nouns I'd studied the night before.* See **decline**.

decline *v.* to inflect a word, or to recite the inflected forms of a word: *Grammar lessons in which the class is asked to decline their nouns and adjectives are a thing of the past, replaced by a new pedagogy stressing language in use.*

decoct   *v.* **1** to extract flavor from something by boiling: *Groncki saved the lobster shells and later decocted an exquisite broth from them.* **2** to concentrate or reduce by boiling: *Decoct the sauce until only a half cup remains.*

decorous   *adj.* dignified; showing good taste: *In contrast to the scandal-ridden stories in the press, the hearings were decorous and businesslike.*

decorticate   *v.* **1** to remove an outer covering from something; peel: *Pie is being made—they're both busy decorticating a bagful of apples and pears.* **2** to remove the cortex from an organ, such as the brain: (fig.) *At 2:00 P.M., a boisterous group, decorticated by beer and camaraderie, had settled in to party under my dorm window.*

defenestration   *n.* the act of throwing someone or something out of a window: *I happened to look out back just in time to see the defenestration of a backpack and pillow from the top-floor apartment.* * (fig.) *Scandal finally led to defenestration of the party's county chairman.*

deference   *n.* respect and courtesy: *Mom always addressed the minister with deference, even when it was to disagree with him.* * *We're having a later dinner this year in deference to our sisters who have a longer distance to travel.*

definite/definitive   see at D CONFUSABLES

delectation *n.* enjoyment and pleasure: *She felt delectation that took the form of near helplessness, like laughter that leaves you weak and almost immobilized.*

delegation see **legation/delegation** at L CONFUSABLES

delegitimatize *v.* to make less legitimate: *Even the appearance of a conflict of interest would delegitimatize his role as a mediator.*

deleterious *adj.* harmful; detrimental: *Not needing to work has a deleterious effect on the rich.*

deliquescent *adj.* melting; becoming soft and liquid: *In one of her more appealing dishes, a deliquescent scoop of sorbet sits in a sea of glistening goo.*

demagogue, demagog *n.* a leader who obtains and keeps power by pandering to public prejudices and by lying about what can and will be achieved: *Some consider Rudy Giuliani a demagogue in mayoral robes.*
  demagogic *adj. These so-called quality-of-life issues tend to take on a demagogic quality, allowing politicians the opportunity to impose their personal vision in the name of the common good.*
  demagoguery *n.* the behavior or methods used by a demagogue: *As he aged, the despot's demagoguery mellowed.*

demarche *n.* **1** an initiative, maneuver, or course of action, especially a diplomatic one: *What sort of demarche could they find to avoid a conflict?* **2** a diplomatic protest: *The European Union sent a demarche* *to the State Department, demanding an end to the sanctions.*

demimonde   *n.* a distinct class or group within society, especially a group that is considered inferior, such as prostitutes, drug users, or transvestites: *I was shocked to learn that Bones knew his way around the New York demimonde I had only read about.*

    demimondain *male,* **demimondaine** *female n.* a habitué of a demimonde: *He was almost ludicrous in appearance but with a dangerous undercurrent that brought to mind a George Grosz demimondain.*

demisemiquaver   *n. esp. British* a thirty-second note

demiurge   *n.* an independent creative force, or a powerful, ruling being: *In the revival of Cabaret, Cumming plays the emcee as a leering, cosmic demiurge who makes it clear that there is no such thing as an innocent bystander.*

demotic   *adj.* of the people, popular, or everyday: *In New York City, preserving gardens created in abandoned building lots by neighborhood people is a demotic issue, and the mayor's efforts to sell these properties is generally despised.*

denature   *v.* to change the nature of something, especially by taking away its original properties: *The island is a denatured country whose wilderness gave way centuries ago to a treeless landscape of densely populated towns and cultivated fields.*

dendrochronology *n.* the scientific comparison of the rings of trees and wood in order to date environmental changes or events: *Samples were taken to an Oxford dendrochronology lab for examination.*

dendrology *n.* the scientific study of trees.
   dendrologist *n. Samples taken by a dendrologist show that the oak roof is one of the oldest in Europe.*

denote see **connote/denote** at C CONFUSABLES

denouement, dénouement *n.* the resolution or final outcome, especially of a dramatic plot, or the point in the plot following the climax where this happens: *The manager was fired last week, and most of the staff left in the denouement.*

deprecate *v.* to make fun of, belittle, or play down the importance of: *Critics are so harsh that you begin to think they'd deprecate Jesus's homilies if he were to make them in a public venue today.* See also **self-deprecating**.

depredation *n.* predatory action or attitude: *This family's depredations constitute a virtual bestiary of abuse.*

deracinate *v.* to uproot or alienate someone from their accustomed environment: *The very act of providing for the refugees deracinates them as they are moved from home, to camp, to another country.*

derivative   *adj.* not original; coming from something else: *The biblical story of Noah appears to be derivative of a passage from the Sumerian epic* Gilgamesh.

dernier cri   *phrase* the last word, or the latest thing: *Williams's* Sweet Bird of Youth *seemed the dernier cri in lurid adult drama when it opened on Broadway in 1959.*

descry   *v.* to notice or discern something far away, or to discover or find something you've been looking for: *I attached the small device to the underside of the car's wheel well, where any random inspection would be unlikely to descry it.*

desecrate   *v.* to profane; to treat in an irreverent or sacrilegious way: *The work is horrible—it disgusts; it desecrates those forced to undertake it.*

desiccated   *adj.* dried up or dehydrated: *The field was littered with desiccated turds that had been dropped by cattle long ago.*

desideratum   *n., pl.* **desiderata** something thought to be necessary or highly desirable: *Is equality a desideratum in a relationship?*
    desiderate   *v.* to consider wanting something, or to express a desire to get something: *For years he had desiderated a country house.*
    desideration   *n. Her desiderations increased almost daily, until it seemed there was nothing she had not expressed interest in acquiring.*

detached see **unattached/detached** at U Confusables

detritus *n.* debris; pieces of worn or discarded material: *Sometimes the artwork displayed in his galleries seems like piles of detritus.*

diaeresis *n., pl.* **diaereses 1** a mark like two dots (¨) placed over the second of two adjacent vowels to show that they are pronounced separately: *Chloë always gets annoyed when people leave the diaeresis off her name.* **2** a break in a line of poetry that happens when the end of a word and the end of a metric foot coincide

diagnosis see at D Confusables

diapason *n.* the full range of sound of a voice or instrument, or a sudden, exclamatory chord that covers such a range of sound: *Silence underscored that scene far more effectively than any diapasons of hyperbolic music ever could.*

diatribe *n.* a bitter, critical attack: *She launched into her usual diatribe about the intolerable lack of consideration drivers show to bicyclists.* Compare **harangue**.

dichotomy *n.* a two-part division: *Once again she faces dichotomy between her desire to study and the need to earn.* Compare **bifurcation**.
    dichotomous *adj.* divided in two, or having two parts: *I'm struck by how dichotomous these prisoner exchanges are—twenty released on one side for one on the other—yet we profess to hold all human beings equal.*

didactic *adj.* inclined to instruct or teach others in an overbearing manner, or used for teaching: *He is not a didactic filmmaker but makes his points with gentle persuasion.* Synonym: **pedantic**.

diffidence *n.* hesitance or lack of self-assurance: *He moved with diffidence, causing others to change direction because they thought he might suddenly turn in their direction.*
    diffident *adj.* shy and reserved: *A diffident presenter is not going to be very convincing. ∗ Don't be taken in by Ben's diffident manner—it's a come-on.*

dilettante *n.* **1** someone with an interest in but only superficial experience or knowledge of art or some particular subject or activity; an amateur: *She's hardly an expert on nineteenth-century literature—more a well-read dilettante.* **2** a lover of the arts; a connoisseur: *a dilettante and collector of contemporary portraiture.*

Dionysiac *adj.* ecstatic, orgiastic, or wild: *New York was long thought to be the center for Dionysiac shenanigans and misbehavior of all sorts.*

In classical mythology, Dionysus was the god of wine, fertility, and drama and was celebrated by an orgiastic religion that honored the power and fertility of nature. Dionysia—festivals—were held in honor of Dionysus. Dionysus is also known as Bacchus, and the Dionysia as Bacchanalia.

disapprobation *n.* disapproval; moral condemnation: *Their disapprobation took us by surprise—we'd expected approval.*

discern *v.* to perceive, recognize, or distinguish something: *As a young man, and even into middle age, he struggled to discern love from lust.*
    discernible *adv.* able to be seen or distinguished: *The new lighting made a discernible improvement in the room's appearance.*
    discernment *n.* the ability to distinguish or discriminate: *I thought her rejection of the offer showed great discernment.*

discomfit *v.* to make someone uneasy: *We'd never met him before, and I was discomfitted by his familiar manner.*

disconsolate *adj.* extremely unhappy and unable to be consoled: *She was disconsolate for days after losing the contest on what she said was an unfair decision.*

discordance *n.* disagreement or conflict; discord: *Developments on the leading edge of medical research can cause discordance between technology and ethics.*

discountenance *v.* to lose one's composure or become embarrassed, or to disturb or embarrass someone: *Steve is not easily discountenanced, but news of the boy's arrest had clearly shaken him.*

discreet see **discrete/discreet** at D CONFUSABLES

discrepant   *adj.* not in agreement; showing a discrepancy: *As theories go, her's does more to cover the discrepant facts than most others that have been proposed.*

discrete see at D CONFUSABLES

disinformation   *n.* deliberately false or misleading information: *The administration put an efficient apparatus in place to spread disinformation and propaganda.*

disingenuous   *adj.* false and insincere: *The offer was disingenuous.* * *They're the two most disingenuous people I've ever met.*
   disingenuously   *adv. Their display of disingenuously correct manners was not lost on our host.*

disinterested see at D CONFUSABLES

disjunction   *n.* a point where something is separated or disconnected: *Between Manhattan's Upper East Side and East Harlem lies Ninety-sixth Street, a disjunction between wealth and poverty.*

dispassionate   *adj.* impartial; unaffected by strong feelings; without passion: *The counsel's testimony was delivered in a dispassionate monotone.*
   dispassionately   *adv. He listened dispassionately to the charges being read.*

dispiriting   *adj.* causing one to feel discouraged or hopeless: *The media feeding frenzy over the foibles of politicians is itself dispiriting.*

disquisition *n.* a formal discussion or piece of writing: *She was impressed by my disquisition on Victorian cooking techniques.*

dissimulate *v.* **1** to hide true motives, intentions, or feelings; pretend: *I'd like to see more of her, but my shyness always causes me to dissimulate.* **2** to conceal the true appearance of someone or something; disguise: *The curls and waves of her hair dissimulate her split ends and uneven cut.*

dissonance *n.* a lack of agreement or accord: *By the time the meeting broke for lunch, it seemed dissonance would lead to impasse.*

distend *v.* to stretch, swell, or spread an elastic container by interior pressure: *I tried not to laugh as water distended the balloon, knowing it would be far too heavy for the kid to pick up, let alone throw.*

distinct/distinctive see at D CONFUSABLES

diurnal *adj.* being active and awake during the day, or happening during the day: *I enjoy getting up at dawn, but believe me, I was less diurnal in my twenties.* ∗ *Few owls are diurnal, most are nocturnal.* See also D CONFUSABLES. Antonym: **nocturnal**.

divagate *v.* to digress from the topic while speaking: *Once he knew what he wanted to say, the doctor could not be made to divagate, but he'd answer questions when he finished his comments.*

divagation *n.* a digression while speaking: *Carol seems to have gone off on another philosophical divagation.*

diversionary *adj.* intended to distract or divert attention away from something: *The owner's claim that the lease is being revoked because of customer complaints is a diversionary tactic—the owner really just wants to rent the space to a friend.*

divination *n.* the foretelling of the future; prophecy or fortune telling: *The I Ching remains a popular personal tool of divination.* Compare **prognostication**.
　divine *v.* **1** to predict or foretell: *I don't know what will happen; I can't divine the future.* **2** to form an opinion or conclusion based on intuition or experience: *I divined negotiations must be underway for a takeover of the company since top management has been so secretive and deeply involved in something.* Compare **prognosticate**; **conjecture**.
　diviner *n.* someone who foretells or predicts. Compare **prognosticator**.

dogmatic *adj.* adhering strictly to an established system of rules and principles: *The situation calls for solutions that are more creative and less dogmatic.*

dominion *n.* complete control and authority: *She could take a drink now and then but had to be careful not to give alcohol dominion over her.*

dominions, dominations *n.* the sixth of nine orders of angels. See THE CELESTIAL HIERARCHY at **angel**.

doppelgänger *n.* a person's double; a ghostly self who is also present on the earth: *My work keeps me too busy—I'll have to get my doppelgänger to find me a girlfriend.*

doughty *adj.* courageous: *The doughty entrepreneur succeeded at a time when a woman in business was rare.*

doyenne *n.* a senior or older woman in a particular class or group: *These women, those from old families and those with new money alike, are the doyennes of Chicago society.* ∗ *a doyenne of the art establishment.*

draconian *adj.* extemely harsh; severe: *While the committee's desire to establish a formal code regarding student behavior during conferences is understandable, are penalties as draconian as those in this draft really necessary?*

dramaturgy *n.* the arts of writing and of producing plays; the theater arts: *The budgetary goings-on in the state legislature too often resemble some existential exercise in dramaturgy.*

dribble see at D CONFUSABLES

drivel see **dribble/drivel** at D CONFUSABLES

droit du seigneur *n.* the right of a feudal lord to have sex with the bride of his vassal on her wedding night, or more broadly, the right of someone who is very important to do as they please: *No one seems to mind* *that this modernist blob of a house has been plopped down among the sedate row houses, perhaps because of the owner's droit du seigneur.*

droll *adj.* amusing in an odd, curious, or unusual way: *I'm never sure if he's joking or not, and his children have the same droll sense of humor.*

dryad *n.* a deity of the forest; a wood nymph in classical mythology: *My girls skipped and played like dryads among the trees.* Compare **hamadryad**.

Spirits, Nymphs, and Mythical Beings

The spirit world brings forth many interesting terms. Some, like *avatar, fata morgana*, and *sybil*, have made the jump to the material world. Others, like *dryad, incubus, kelpie,* and *peri*, have remained more elusive, but offer enjoyable alternatives to the shopworn *spirit*.

Avatar *n.* the embodiment of something, or a personification. In Hinduism, an avatar is the incarnation of a deity. Hindu literature relates several incarnations of the Hindu deity Vishnu, most notably as the avatar Krishna in the Bhagavad-Gita, and as each of the three Ramas in the Ramayana.

Chimera *n.* a fire-breathing creature in classical mythology that has the head of a lion, a goat's body, and a dragon's tail.

Cimmerian *n.* one of the mythical people described by Homer as inhabiting a remote land of darkness.

dryad *n.* a deity of the forest; a wood nymph in classical mythology.

fata morgana *n.* a mirage in which visual distortions make cliffs or buildings appear to be elaborate castles, or any mirage involving visual distortion. *Fata morgana* is Latin and Italian for Morgan le Fay, who in Celtic myth and Arthurian legend is a goddess, priestess, fairy, or sorceress.

hamadryad *n.* a wood nymph in classical mythology who inhabits a particular tree and dies when the tree does.

incubus *n.* a devil in the form of a man which in medieval times was believed to have sex with a sleeping woman.

kelpie *n.* a creature in Scottish folklore who causes travelers to drown.

numen *n.* a spirit, especially one considered to inhabit particular parts of nature or objects.

peri *n.* a being in Persian mythology who descended from fallen angels and was excluded from Paradise until its penance was completed.

sibyl *n.* a woman who can tell the future, especially one of up to ten women living in different parts of the ancient world who were thought to be able to foretell the future, the most famous of which was the source of the Sibylline Books, which prophesied Rome's destiny and which were burned in 83 B.C.

succubus *n.* a devil in the form of a woman which in medieval times was believed to have sex with a sleeping man.

duress *n.* pressure through threat or force; coercion: *The agreement was signed under duress and should be declared invalid.*

dyeing/dying see at D CONFUSABLES

dysphemism *n.* the substitution of an offensive or disparaging statement for an inoffensive or agreeable one, or this type of statement: *He uses dysphemism just to irritate me.*

dystopian *adj.* extremely depressing; grim; oppressive: *We were appalled by the dystopian neglect of the neighborhood's once handsome, respectable buildings by greedy, irresponsible landlords.*
　　dystopia *n.* a hypothetical, oppressive state or society, usually characterized by squalor, terror, and deprivation, or a story about such a place: *the dystopia of* Fahrenheit 451
　　Antonyms: **utopian**; **utopia**.

E

CONFUSABLES

eager/anxious See **anxious/eager** at A CON-FUSABLES

economic/economical Both words mean thrifty (*an economic/economical vacation*); *economic* also means pertaining to an economy or economics (*an economic nightmare*), or profitable (*an economic windfall*).

effect/affect See **affect/effect** at A CONFUSABLES

egregious/outstanding/exceptional *Egregious* means remarkably bad (*an egregious lapse in judgment*); *outstanding* means conspicuous (*an outstanding effort*); *exceptional* can mean superior (*exceptional intelligence*) or notably above or below average (*Both are exceptional* *students, but one needs tutoring while the other could be a tutor.*).

elusive/illusive Something *elusive* is physically hard to grasp (*Snakes can be pretty elusive.*), hard to understand (*Math can be an elusive subject.*), or hard to identify (*The cause of this syndrome has remained elusive.*); something *illusive* is deceptive or based on deception (*I fell for that illusive ad claiming I could retire in three years.*).

emigrate/immigrate To *emigrate* is to leave a country to live elsewhere (*My family emigrated from Ghana twelve years ago.*); to *immigrate* is to come to a country to live (*My family immigrated to the United States in the 1980s.*).

eminent/imminent Something *eminent* stands out or displays superior qualities (*an eminent scholar*); something *imminent* is about to happen (*an imminent storm*).

empathy/sympathy *Empathy* is the experience of sharing someone else's feelings (*Having lost a child to cancer, I have great empathy for other parents whose children develop cancer.*); *sympathy* is understanding of or concern for someone else's feelings (*Although my parents are still alive, I have great sympathy for people whose parents have died.*).

endemic/epidemic *Endemic* means particular to a place or population (*Malaria is endemic to tropical regions.*); *epidemic* means spreading rapidly within a place or population (*AIDS is epidemic in parts of Africa.*).

enervate/energize To *enervate* is to dissipate or lessen (*This job enervates me to the point where I can barely get home before falling asleep.*); to *energize* is to enliven or invigorate (*That vacation energized me.*).

environment/habitat See **habitat/environment** at H CONFUSABLES

epicure/gastronome/gourmet All three words describe someone who is knowledgeable about and enjoys good food and drink. An *epicure* is careful about what is consumed and takes great enjoyment in consuming it; a *gastronome* knows the history and cultural importance of what's being eaten; a *gourmet* tends to be discriminating and to enjoy knowing about the subtleties of what's on the table. See also **gourmet/gourmand** at G CONFUSABLES.

epigram/epigraph An *epigram* is a witty or wise saying (*He came up with the epigram "Drunk driving can kill a friendship."*); an *epigraph* is a quotation given at the beginning of a literary work that is meant to set the tone for what follows (*She used some very inappropriate epigraph from* Ulysses.).

epithet/epitaph An *epithet* is a word or phrase that characterizes or disparages someone (*We used the epithet "Mr. Fun" for our dour biology teacher.*); an *epitaph* is an inscription on a tombstone (*I'd like my epitaph to read, "I told you I was sick."*).

epithet/curse An *epithet* is a word or phrase that characterizes or disparages someone (*We used the epithet "Mr. Fun" for our dour biology teacher.*); a *curse* is an invocation of evil, or abusive profanity (*She put a curse on the king's household for seven generations to come.*).

essay/assay see **assay/essay** at A CONFUSABLES

ethical/moral Both words describe what is good rather than bad. *Ethical* deals with professional standards or what is thought to be good by a group or organization (*Professors must be ethical in their dealings with students.*); *moral* deals with an individual's judgment or choices about what is right, or with what is considered good by religious teachings or social beliefs (*She opposes nuclear weapons on moral grounds.*).

evoke/invoke *Evoke* means to bring to mind (*Her picture evokes memories of a very happy time.*), or to produce (*I could not evoke so much as a giggle from that audience.*); *invoke* means to call upon (*to invoke the forgiveness* *of the Lord*), or to implement (*to invoke emergency powers granted under the War Powers Act*); both words can mean to conjure (*evoke a spell*), or to cite approvingly (*Pan-Africanists invoked the writings of Kwame Nkrumah*), although *invoke* is preferred for these senses.

excuse/pardon see **pardon/excuse** at P CON-FUSABLES

exotic/esoteric *Exotic* means very strange or unusual (*Lions are in danger of becoming exotic even in Kenya*); *esoteric* means known or understood by only a few (*the esoteric writings of Madam Blavatsky*)

---

eager see **anxious/eager** at A CONFUSABLES

ebb *v.* to flow back, decline, or fade away: *The populace was cheered and celebrated when the victorious rebels marched into the capital, but their exhilaration quickly ebbed.*
   ebb, ebb tide *n.* the outgoing flow of the sea: *the ocean's ebb and flow*

ebullient *adj.* excitedly happy; bubbling with enthusiasm: *His normally ebullient mood would go through a marked seasonal dip around mid-December.*
   ebullience *n.* enthusiasm: *Their initial ebullience wore off when they saw exactly how much work was involved.*

economic/economical see at E CONFUSABLES

ectomorph *n.* a tall, thin person: *I felt like a squat little dumpling placed among the ectomorphs of the basketball team.*
  ectomorphic *adj. His ectomorphic physique intimidated even people who were much stronger than he was.*

ecumenist *n.* someone who promotes unity among different factions of a group or organization, especially among different religious denominations: *His faith in the basic goodness of humanity marks him as an ecumenist, as one who searches for common ground.*
  ecumenism *n.* unity among various factions, or efforts to achieve unity: *The ecumenism that marked official Roman Catholic policy beginning in the mid-60s met with some well-publicized successes, and a few quiet failures.*

edify *v.* to instruct, enlighten, and uplift: *Unlike most conference sessions, which seem to be something to endure, this one edified its audience in surprising ways.*

educe *v.* to bring out, discover, or deduce something: *I tried to educe some spark, some sign of life in Michael's stultifying personality.* Synonym: **elicit**.

efface *v.* **1** to remove or rub out: *I developed an affection for them that subsequent events did nothing to efface.* **2** to make yourself unnoticed or unnoticeable: *Not wanting to disturb their fun, I effaced my-self by sitting quietly in the corner until it was time to leave.*

effect see **affect/effect** at A Confusables

effervescent   *adj.* **1** lively and enthusiastic: *This band's effervescent music may not be for everybody, but these twelve-year-olds were clearly enjoying it.* Synonym: **vivacious**. **2** having and giving off bubbles: *All I want is a tall glass of cold, effervescent water.*
   effervescence   *n.* **1** *Julie's effervescence is contagious.* **2** *It's the sparkling wine's effervescence that I don't like!*

effete   *adj.* depleted, overrefined and self-indulgent, or decadent: *The novel is set during the final century of effete rule as the Roman Empire lost its power and its provinces.* ∗ *an effete snob*

efficacious   *adj.* effective in causing or producing a particular effect: *They marketed the snake oil as an efficacious remedy for everything from headaches to boils.*
   efficacy, efficacity   *n.* effectiveness in producing, usually a particular effect: *The efficacity of a fish's pelvic fins has never been matched by the various stabilizing devices used on ships.*

efflorescence   *n.* a dry coating, crust, or powder: *Blood formed a wine-colored efflorescence on her lip.*

effluent   *n.* a liquid outflow, especially of waste water or sewage: *The PCBs entered the river in an effluent containing industrial wastes discharged by companies upstream.* Compare **effluvia**.

effluvia   *n.* waste matter or by-products: *If the world is to survive the postindustrial age, we must find a way to protect it from our effluvia.* Although effluvia is the plural form of the singular **effluvium**, it is more commonly used in singular constructions, especially as a mass noun. Compare **effluent**.

effusion   *n.* a flow or outpouring of something: *Never was there such an effusion of guilt and remorse.*

effusive   *adj.* overly enthusiastic: *A newborn's parents can, perhaps, be forgiven if their praise of their progeny flirts with the effusive.* Synonym: **fulsome**.

egis   *n.* see at **aegis**.

egregious   *adj.* extreme, especially in being bad, offensive, or unpleasant: *The egregious inequality of Microsoft's position in the computer industry had competitors howling for relief from the Justice Department.* See at E Confusables

eleemosynary   *adj.* having to do with or supported by charity: *Michelle's eleemosynary works include a weekly stint at the local soup kitchen.*

elegy   *n.* a song or poem with a sad, contemplating tone, especially one suitable or written for the dead: *She wrote a moving elegy in honor of her son, who had died so young.* Compare **eulogy**.

    elegiac *adj.* having a sad or mournful character or tone; suitable for a funeral: *The autumnal barbecue had an elegiac note, bringing into focus the fact that summer was well and truly over.*

elicit *v.* to bring out or find out something by encouraging someone: *We haven't been able to elicit cooperation from the residents of the building.* Synonym: **educe**.

    elicitor *n. Deirdre was an elicitor, someone who made conversation flow effortlessly with even the most reticent.*

elide *v.* to leave out or omit something: *In editing the story, you elided a crucial part of the plot.* See also **elision**. Compare **excise**.

elision *n.* an omission, or the act of leaving out something, such as a letter in a word, a thought, or a step in a process: *The elision of their names in later editions of the catalogue was taken as an intentional slight.* * *Convenient elisions in the flow of information helped sow the bitter discords of the Cold War.* See also **elide**.

elucidate *v.* to make something clear or to give an explanation: *Professor Vizard's efforts to elucidate the causes of this conflict have failed to help me make sense of it.* * *Could you please elucidate?*

elusive see at E CONFUSABLES

emancipate *v.* to release from a social or legal restraint, or to free from bondage; liberate: *She longed to be emancipated from the strictures and intrigues of office politics.*
  emancipation *n. June dragged on while the kids longed for their summer emancipation. * Some slave owners provided for the emancipation of their slaves in their wills.*
  Compare **manumit**; **manumission**.

embouchure *n.* the position of the mouth when blowing into a wind instrument: *He practiced every day, even on weekends, making his fingers memorize their positions and his mouth memorize its embouchure.*

emendation *n.* a correction or change made, usually to a text: *Several emendations have been made to the new edition.*

emigrate see at E CONFUSABLES

eminent see at E CONFUSABLES

emoticon *n.* a figure used especially in e-mail which is typed on a keyboard using punctuation symbols to represent an emotion such as happiness, sadness, or confusion: *She signs her e-mail with an insipid smiley emoticon that's winking at you:* ;).

empathy *n.* the ability to identify with the feelings of another person: *Her self-centeredness stems from an almost total lack of empathy.* See at E CONFUS-ABLES

    empathetic, **empathic** *adj. An empathetic listener functions as a sort of antidepressant.*

empyrean *n.* a perfect place or state, or heaven: *Take solace in the fact that he is in a better place, an empyrean enfolding him in everlasting love.*

    empyreal *adj. We were astounded to see that Jeanne had transformed her East Village hovel into an empyreal home.*

emulate *v.* to copy or imitate: *She tries to emulate her older sister.*

    emulation *n.* the act of imitating or copying: *Emulation can be seen as a way of maintaining traditions so they are passed to future generations.*

emulsify *v.* to combine one liquid with another through which it can be dispersed in suspension but not fully blended: *Mustard can be used to help emulsify oil and vinegar. * Their tastes become emulsified, like ingredients in mayonnaise.*

encomium *n., pl.* **encomiums**, **encomia** praise, a tribute: *The poem "Ode to O. D." is an encomium to Ruby Dee's husband, Ossie Davis. * "She's a woman who really knows how to laugh"—the perfect encomium for a comedian's spouse.*

endemic *adj.* **1** always present in a population but usually controlled: *Malaria, endemic in much of*

Central America, was devastating to North Americans working on construction of the Panama Canal, who had never before been exposed to the disease. **2** common or particular to a place or a group of people: *an endemic species.* See at E CONFUSABLES. Compare **epidemic**; **pandemic**.

endogamy   *n.* marriage only within a particular group: *Members of the church practiced endogamy.*
   endogamous   *adj. Among many seventeenth-century religious groups marriage was strictly endogamous.*
   Antonyms: **exogamy, exogamous**.

endoskeleton   *n.* the internal skeleton of a body or, figuratively, the internal framework of something: *We turned a corner, entering a part of the complex where the wallboard wasn't installed yet, and found ourselves within the endoskeleton of what would be the dining hall.*
   endoskeletal   *adj. I'm amazed again by the sight of the graceful, endoskeletal ribs that have supported the massive roof of this cathedral for so many centuries.*

energize see **enervate/energize** at E CONFUSABLES

enervate see at E CONFUSABLES

engender   *v.* to produce or cause to exist: *His interest in promoting baseball internationally was engendered when his family accompanied the Dodgers to Japan for an exhibition series.*

enmity *n.* hostility; hatred that is often mutual: *They can't work together at all—their enmity causes too many problems.* * *Nationalistic enmities could lead to war.*

ennui *n.* a feeling of tiredness and boredom: *A well-known socialite, she would sometimes suffer ennui at even the thought of yet another party.*

entomological *adj.* relating to the study of insects: *I'm afraid my entomological pursuits this summer were confined to ridding the rafters of a wasp nest and the patio of an ant colony.*

entropic see at **entropy**.

entropy *n.* **1** the hypothetical tendency of the universe to evolve toward an inert and uniform state: *The lecture touched on the big bang, entropy, and chaos theory.* * *Physics reveals that time may tend toward entropy.* **2** the inevitable decline of any social system or society: *Modern life is an accumulation of facts without knowledge, bringing us entropy rather than enlightenment.*
> **entropic** *adj. We think of museums as static institutions, not as entropic organizations that are continually decaying and must renew themselves.*

entr'acte *n.* an intermission between acts of a play, something performed during an intermission, or music played before the beginning of the next act, especially of a musical: *We considered leaving* *during the intermission, but then the entr'acte started and we made the unfortunate decision to stay.*

enunciate *v.* **1** to state, declare, or announce something: *In 1918, Woodrow Wilson enunciated the right of self-determination for the peoples of the Ottoman and Austro-Hungarian empires.* **2** to pronounce clearly: *You must enunciate the words when you sing.*

environment see **habitat/environment** at H CON-FUSABLES

eolian, aeolian *adj.* having to do with, caused by, or carried on the wind: *The eolian spores can travel for thousands of miles, and even cross the oceans.*

ephebe, ephebus *n., pl.* **ephebes, ephebi** a young person: *Every fall, Michelle faces the ignorant ephebes who people her freshman comp class, hoping that at least one of them will evince a little interest in improving their skills.*

In ancient Athens, an ephebus was a young man training to become a full citizen.

---

epicure *n.* someone with a very refined taste for food and drink who greatly enjoys eating and drinking the finest: *I'm surprised to find an epicure such as you eating in a greasy spoon like this.* See at E CONFUSABLES. Compare **gourmand.**

epicurean *adj.* very fancy and refined in taste: *She's got this epicurean approach to food shopping where she can only buy fruit in this place, and vegetables someplace else, and coffee at a little importer's, and bread at a special bakery.*

epidemic *n.* **1** a disease spreading rapidly throughout a community: *The flu epidemic has spread into nearby states.* **2** something that has spread or increased rapidly or suddenly: *An epidemic of downsizing has taken hold in high-tech companies in the northeast.*
    epidemic *adj.* happening quickly or affecting many: *an epidemic virus* ∗ *Distrust of politicians had reached epidemic proportions among voters nationwide.*
    See **endemic/epidemic** at E CONFUSABLES. Compare **endemic; pandemic**.

epigone, epigon *n.* an imitator, follower, or successor of an artist: *The doctor is an epigone of the surrealists—it's his avocation.* ∗ *The authenticity of the work hasn't been established, and it may be the work of one of his epigones.*

epigram/epigraph see at E CONFUSABLES

epiphany *n.* a sudden insight or intuition: *A good mystery should elicit discomfort and perhaps a bit of fear, and provide a few well-crafted epiphanies.*
    epiphanic, epiphanous *adj. You can almost feel the presence of the past when you walk in, as though an epiphanic aura were exerting itself on your consciousness.*

epistemology *n.* the philosophical study of the nature of knowledge: *The author describes his investigations into crimes committed by children and the attendant epistemology, asking, Can these children truly know what they have done or what their punishment will mean?*

   epistemological *adj.* relating to the philosophical investigation of the nature of knowledge: *This English teacher's methods reflected an epistemological approach that seemed more appropriate for a younger age group.*

epithet see **epithet/curse**; **epithet/epitaph** at E Confusables

epitaph see **epithet/epitaph** at E Confusables

epitome *n.* the best example of something: *Spending hundreds of dollars for toilet seats was considered the epitome of Pentagon wastefulness.*

epitomize *v.* to be a typical example: *The failure of good intentions is epitomized eloquently by the decaying public housing dotting the landscape.*

epoch *n.* a particular time period, or a point in time marking a historical period: *An epoch of peace under the "new world order" so talked of after the demise of the Communist states has remained elusive at best.* ∗ *The company is entering a new epoch with expansion into international markets.*

   epochal *adj.* significant or important: *The development of the steam engine was an epochal event.* ∗

The latter half of the twentieth century has seen epochal changes in the conduct and regulation of international trade.

eponym *n.* the person from whom something takes its name: *Escherichia coli is commonly called E. coli, and its eponym is Theodor Escherich.* Compare **toponym**.

    eponymous, eponymic *adj.* named for or thought to have been named for a párticular person: *The program will examine the eponymous fashion and perfume business of Coco Chanel.*

    eponymously *adv. Steve and Jamie are co-owners of the eponymously named law firm of Fishman and Neil.*

Eponymous Words

Eponyms are words that derive from the names of people. The names of these things or events are unusual in that they are not rooted in any linguistic history, but instead have sprung fully formed from the names of people involved in their creation or popularization. In addition to the very common terms that most people know, such as *Halley's Comet* and *John Hancock*, there are a number of surprising eponyms.

ampere *n.* the base unit of measurement of electrical current. Named for André Marie Ampère, a nineteenth-century French physicist.

bowie knife *n.* a type of hunting knife which has a back edge that is curved and sharpened. Named for James Bowie, a Texas landowner who was killed at the Alamo.

boycott *n.* an organized effort to change business or social practices by refusing to participate in an activity, use a service, or buy goods at a particular place. Named for Charles C. Boycott, a nineteenth-century English estate manager in Ireland who was subjected to such tactics when he refused to reduce rents.

Cliffs Notes *n. trademark* a series of study aids that summarize literary works. Named for Cliff Hillegas, who originated the series.

dunce *n.* a stupid or foolish person. Named for John Duns Scotus, a thirteenth-century Scottish theologian whose once-accepted writings were attacked as foolish by sixteenth-century satirists.

Ferris wheel *n.* an upright wheel with seats that carry people around the wheel's outer edge. Named for G. W. G. Ferris, a nineteenth-century American engineer.

Hansard *n.* the official published report of parliamentary proceedings and debates in a British Commonwealth nation. The report is named for Luke Hansard, a nineteenth-century British printer.

hertz *n.* a unit of frequency used to measure waves. Named for the nineteenth-century German physicist Heinrich Rudolph Hertz.

Mason jar *n.* a type of jar with a sealable lid. Patented by John M. Mason in 1858.

Occam's razor *n.* the principle that the fewest number of assumptions should be made in trying to explain or understand something, or that the simplest explanation is the most likely. The principle was developed by the fourteenth-century philosopher William of Occam.

ohm *n.* a unit of electrical resistance. Named for the nineteenth-century German physicist George Simon Ohm.

Ponzi scheme *n.* a financial swindle in which the investment capital of new investors is used to pay off previous investors until the scheme collapses because there are no new investors. The swindle is named for Charles Ponzi, who made $15,000,000 from it in 1920.

rickey *n.* a drink made with lime juice and soda water and sometimes also with gin. Dating from the late nineteenth century and attributed to a Colonel Rickey.

saxophone *n.* any of a family of wind instruments with reeds. Named for nineteenth-century Belgian instrument maker Antoine Sax.

equable   *adj*. unvarying, uniform, or without extreme changes: *The last speaker's soft, modulated, equable voice actually—and embarrassingly—put me to sleep.*

equanimity   *n*. composure, or calmness in a stressful situation: *I'm glad to see Ellen's usual equanimity has returned—she was so stressed out the last time we saw her.* * *She heard him out with studied equanimity.*

equanimous   *adj*. being unruffled or untroubled: *He wore one of those equanimous mustaches that look too good to have been grown by ordinary means.*

equipoise   *n*. balance, or an equal distribution of something; equilibrium: *The wordplay, diction, and syntax of these songs had an equipoise that contrasted with the social self-consciousness of the bedeviled singer.*

equitation   *n*. the art of riding a horse, or the riding itself: *A problem with this stable is the poor equitation of some of the riders here.*

equivocal   *adj*. having or accepting more than one opinion or meaning: *I look for decisive employees, and her equivocal statements in the interview make me think she is not what I am looking for.*

equivocate *v.* to be ambiguous, or to avoid taking a definite position: *He doesn't equivocate, and doesn't like people who do.*

equivocation *n. If you continue with these constant equivocations, you'll find the decisions have been made anyway and you'll have no choice at all.*

eremite *n.* a recluse or hermit, especially a religious hermit: *The road isn't passable most of the winter, but that doesn't matter to the eremite who lives up there.*

eremitic *adj. an eremitic lifestyle*

eremitism *n. The people in town are accustomed to the eremitism of the monks.*

Eros *n.* **1** sexual desire: *Eros has gotten him in trouble once again.* **2** *pl.* **Erotes** a statue or other representation of the god Eros: *a collection of Erotes.*

In classical mythology, Eros is the god of love.

erudite *adj.* knowledgeable, fully educated, and sophisticated: *An erudite inventor, he has developed some of the more sophisticated toys on the market today.*

esculent *adj.* edible; usable as food: *Some of the things on this plate are barely esculent.*

esculence *n.* the quality of being edible or of being worth eating: *This dish has the highest degree of esculence, delicacy, and artistry.*

esoteric *adj.* understood or used by only a small group, especially by people with particular knowledge or training: *Before the AIDS epidemic, the immune system was a pretty esoteric area of medicine.* See **exotic/esoteric** at E CONFUSABLES.

essay see **assay/essay** at A CONFUSABLES

esthete *n.* see at **aesthete.**

ethical see at E CONFUSABLES

ethnography *n.* the study and description of human cultures: *Mead's work changed the face of ethnography.*
    ethnographic, ethnographical *adj.* having to do with the study of human culture: *He argues that there is no evidence of cannibalism in the ethnographic record.*

ethos *n.* the characteristic beliefs and attitudes of a person or group: *Their pessimism is just one manifestation of the ethos of hopelessness that overwhelms this community.*

etiolate *v.* to become pale and weak (used especially of a plant): *Lack of water will etiolate even the hardiest species.*
    etiolated *adj. The only thing left in the house was an etiolated poinsettia.*

etiology *n.* the determination or assignment of a cause of something, the cause itself, or the study of causation: *The course focuses on the etiology of revolution.* ∗ *Just now, the etiology of the company's financial problems is less important than a solution.*

etymon   *n.* 1 an earlier form of a word in the same language or in a language from which it developed: *The Old English word* twa *is an etymon of* two. 2 a word or part of a word from which compounds and derivatives are formed: *The Greek word* eu *means "well," and is an etymon of* euphemism. 3 a foreign word from which a given loanword is derived: *The French word* femme *comes from the Latin etymon* femina.

euhemerism   *n.* the interpretation of myths as stories about historically true events and real people.
  euhemeristic *adj. She gives a euhemeristic spin to the tale of Romulus and Remus.*

eulogy   *n.* a speech or statement praising someone, especially one who has died: *Mike delivered a stirring eulogy for his brother-in-law, after which there was not a dry eye in the house.* Compare **elegy.**

euphoria   *n.* a feeling of great happiness and well-being: *The doctor warned that the antidepressant could cause a false sense of euphoria.*
  euphoric   *adj. Cory was euphoric after winning the piano competition.*

eutrophication   *n.* the process in which a lake becomes too full of nutrients, causing plants to grow excessively, which in turn depletes the water's oxygen and kills off fish: *Marj had studied the eutrophication of lakes in the Adirondacks.*

evanescent *adj.* tending to fade away or disappear quickly; fleeting: *She let out a giddy, evanescent giggle that I found a bit weird.* Synonym: **fugacious.**

   evanescence *n. The evanescence of a raucous New Year's Eve quickly gave way to the cold reality of another Monday morning.*

eviscerate *v.* **1** to remove the essential parts of something: *The review committee eviscerated my project plan, and frankly, I don't see any reason to proceed with this program.* **2** to disembowel: *The pheasants were eviscerated and left hanging in a row.*

evoke see at E CONFUSABLES

exceptional see **egregious/outstanding/exceptional** at E CONFUSABLES

excise *v.* to cut out or remove: *It was agreed to excise paragraph three from the contract.* * *I'll never be able to excise the memory of his terrible fall.* Compare **elide.**

excoriate *v.* to denounce: *Referring to the unfavorable representations of him in the press, he proclaimed, "I have been pilloried and excoriated."*

exculpate *v.* to clear someone of blame, or show that someone is not guilty of wrongdoing: *A review* *of the records failed to exculpate senior corporate officers of conspiracy to defraud.*

    exculpatory *adj.* showing someone to be blameless or free of guilt: *All the evidence we've seen is exculpatory.*

excursus *n.* a long appendix or digression that gives more information or details about a particular topic or point: *After a painstakingly detailed excursus on the history of fossil-hunting, he returns to the much more interesting account of how he discovered these fossils.*

excuse see **pardon/excuse** at P CONFUSABLES

exegesis *n., pl.* **exegeses** an explanation, critical analysis, or interpretation, usually of a text: *The proposed agreement is fully annotated, with an exegesis by the reviewer at the beginning of each section.*

    exegete, exegetist *n.* a textual analyst: *The fragments will be read into the computer system so they can be accessed by exegetes at several different sites.*

    exegetic, exegetical *adj.* of a text, explanatory or critical: *The book is essentially an exegetical work.*

exhortation *n.* an urgent warning or appeal; earnest advice: *My exhortations did nothing to change her mind.*

exigency   *n.* something urgent, or an emergency: *Apple drove from Wisconsin to New Jersey with the three children, bringing along a cell phone should any exigency arise.*

     exigencies   *pl. n.* that which is required in a particular situation: *I'm worried about her ability to cope with the exigencies of caring for a newborn.*

existential   *adj.* of the nature of existence, especially as expressed in the philosophy of existentialism, or relating to dread, distress, or reluctance involving the consequences of one's choices: *Jeanne said our seven year old was up half the night having an existential crisis over the problem of having friends on two continents an ocean apart.* ∗ *an existential dilemma*

exogamy   *n.* marriage outside of a particular group: *The Quakers accepted exogamy in 1860.*

     exogamous   *n. In spite of their religious upbringing, the marriages of all but two of the ten were exogamous.*

     Antonyms: **endogamy, endogamous.**

exophthalmic   *adj.* having eyes that bulge out abnormally: *Theresa's exophthalmic appearance gave you the impression she was constantly startled.*

exotic/esoteric see at E CONFUSABLES

expatriate   *n.* someone living in a foreign country: *Harold has spent the last fifteen years of his life as an expatriate in New Zealand.*

expeditious *adj.* prompt; quickly and efficiently done: *We received an expeditious reply.*

    expeditiously *adv. The closing on the house was expeditiously handled.*

expiate *v.* to atone or make amends for a wrongdoing: *She only hoped to expiate in time for the troubles her addiction had brought her family.*

    expiatory *adj. Lenny is what you might call a player, and when he steps on yet another woman's heart, he employs flowers as part of an expiatory ritual—dumping her gently.*

    expiation *n.* atonement or reparation: *He offered his sacrifices to God in expiation for his sins. * The perpetrators felt their crimes required neither explanation nor expiation.*

explicate *v.* to examine or explain in detail: *I tried to explicate the meaning of habitual behavior, investing it with psychological bric-a-brac and socio-cultural import.*

    explication *n. After much study and reflection, I came up with an explication, or more correctly, with a number of explications, each having at least some validity.*

exponential *adj.* multiplying or increasing in a dramatic way: *The exponential increase in the student population led to severe classroom overcrowding.*

    exponentially *adv.* increasing dramatically as though multiplied by itself many times: *The expo-*

nentially expanding power of circuit-based computers can't continue forever.

expropriate *v.* to take something, usually property, from someone or for someone: *Privately held land and businesses were expropriated for public use.*

F

CONFUSABLES

farther/further Both words have to do with additional distance. *Farther* is generally used for physical distance (*moving farther from home*); *further* is more usual when describing a figurative distance (*The two sides are further apart than ever.*).

faze/phase *Faze* is a verb meaning to disrupt or bother (*The steady drip from the leaky faucet started to faze me.*); *phase* can be used as a verb meaning to introduce (*They phased in the new regulations.*) or eliminate (*to phase out a product line*); as a noun, a *phase* is one part or segment (*the phases of the moon*) or a stage of development (*All kids go through that phase.*).

feasible/possible *Feasible* means likely, reasonable, or practical to carry out (*It's not feasible* *to walk from Maine to California.*); *possible* means able to be carried out given the right circumstances (*It is possible to walk from Maine to California.*).

flagrant/blatant see **blatant/flagrant** at B CON-FUSABLES

flail/flay To *flail* is to hit or move as if hitting with a thresher (*flail about in the water*); to *flay* is to skin (*flay a deer*), to lash (*The headmaster flayed the boy for speaking out of turn.*), or to criticize severely (*She really lit into him, flaying him for his bad taste, his low reputation, and his crummy character.*).

flair/flare *Flair* is skill or talent (*a flair for dramatics*) or style (*dressing with flair*); a *flare* is a burning light (*emergency flares*), an outburst (*a flare of temper*), or a part that spreads outward (*the flare at the mouth of a vase*).

flatulence/afflatus see **afflatus/flatulence** at A CONFUSABLES

flaunt/flout To *flaunt* something is to display it ostentatiously (*When you've got it, flaunt it.*); to *flout* something is to treat it with contempt (*to flout the school rules*).

flotsam/jetsam Usually cojoined in the phrase *flotsam and jetsam* to mean miscellaneous material or vagrant people. *Flotsam* is floating

debris (*Flotsam from the wreck made naviga-*
tion tricky.); *jetsam* is cargo jettisoned in an
effort to save a sinking ship (*The beach was
littered with jetsam.*).

flounder/founder To *flounder* is to move clum-
sily (*He drunkenly floundered his way home.*),
or to seek a foothold with difficulty (*Climbers
floundered along the rocky ledge.*); to *founder*
is to become disabled or sink (*Our little boat
foundered on the rocks.*), or to fail (*Her business foundered when recession struck.*).

forbear/forebear To *forbear* an activity is to
refrain from it or stop doing it (*I must ask you
to forbear smoking.*); a *forebear* (also spelled
forbear) is an ancestor (*Our forebears set forth
the Declaration of Independence.*).

fortunate/fortuitous A *fortunate* event or occurrence is characterized by unexpected good
results (*It was fortunate we met this morning.*);
a *fortuitous* event or occurrence is unplanned
and may be good or bad (*A fortuitous meeting
on the street led to a fistfight.*).

fulsome/bountiful If something is *fulsome* it
is offensive or excessive and insincere (*Your
flattery is fulsome praise.*); if something is
bountiful, it is abundant (*a bountiful harvest*).

---

fabricate   *v.* **1** to create or construct: *The older students were in charge of fabricating the set.* **2** to make

up, invent, or fake something such as a lie, story, or document: *Bill fabricates his own fairy stories.* * *I wouldn't believe anything he told you—he's always fabricating some story.*

fabulist *n.* a creator of fables, or more broadly, a liar: *To compensate for a lack of attention at home, Inge became a showoff and a talented fabulist.*

facetious *adj.* playfully and usually inappropriately humorous, amusing, or frivolous: *At the risk of sounding facetious, the proposal for one reporter to cover "the crime of the century" seems inadequate.*

factitious *adj.* contrived, artificial, lacking spontaneity: *The forced gaiety and factitious laughter of cocktail parties depresses me.*

factotum *n.* an employee having a variety of responsibilities, usually someone's assistant: *Although he was also a team owner, some thought of Selig as the factotum of White Sox chief Jerry Reinsdorf.*

fallacious *adj.* based on a false notion or incorrect reasoning; misleading: *I tried farming out some of the work under the fallacious assumption that any avid reader could abridge a book.*

farouche *adj.* wild and untamed: *He admired the expressive, farouche beauty of Mary's eyes.*

farther see at F Confusables

fascicle *n.* a bundle, especially the gathered papers of a small piece of writing, which combined with other writings forms a larger work; a section of a book published as a separate piece, or a book in a set published as a separate volume: *Dickinson left most of her poems in sheets of paper she sewed together herself in a series of fascicles.*

fastidious *adj.* very painstaking and particular: *He shared his father's fastidious distaste for decorative froufrou.*

fata morgana, **Fata Morgana** *n.* *(Latin/Italian; Morgan le Fay)* a mirage in which visual distortions make cliffs or buildings appear to be elaborate castles, or any mirage involving visual distortion: *The dream had the quality of a fata morgana. * I was still dizzy, and when I turned my head a fata morgana appeared.*

> In Celtic mythology and Arthurian legend, Morgan le Fay is a goddess, priestess, fairy, or sorceress.

fatuous *adj.* inanely foolish and stupid: *That movie is another of those fatuous, bubblegum comedies.*
    fatuity *n.* *The fatuity of the meeting was beyond belief.*

fauna *n., pl.* **faunas, faunae** the animals of a particular region: *Sixteenth-century explorers brought* *the fauna of Europe to the Americas to ensure themselves a supply of familiar food.*

faze see at F CONFUSABLES

fealty *n.* faithfulness or fidelity: *The other programmers looked on Alan as mentor and guru to whom they gladly gave their fealty, and when he left, they went with him.*

feasible see at F CONFUSABLES

febrile *adj.* intensely emotional or intensely active; feverish: *Through the long, lonely nights, my febrile imagination was stalked by the specter of death.*

feckless *adj.* weak, lazy, or irresponsible: *Dad would never tolerate the feckless, it's-not-my-fault approach that Tom often took when things did not go well.*

fecund *adj.* ready and able to reproduce; fertile: *She had the broad, rounded buttocks of a robust and fecund woman.*
    fecundity *n. I sat in the obstetrician's waiting room, surrounded on all sides by clear evidence of fecundity.*

felicitous *adj.* appropriate or suitable: *Almost everything he wrote was inimical to felicitous intergroup relations—his characters were rapacious*

Jews, no-account blacks, shrewish housewives, and the like.

feral *adj.* wild, untamed, or undomesticated: *These feral pigs are descended from domesticated stock left here by seventeenth-century European explorers.* ∗ *(fig.) a gang of feral youths*

ferment *n.* unrest, commotion, and excitement: *The level of ferment suggests this is a movie of uncommon social insight.*

fervent *adj.* with great emotion or enthusiasm: *He has a fervent conviction about the value of music education.* Synonym: **ardent**.

fervid *adj.* impassioned; vehement or intense: *My memories of those fervid days of the student strike remain vivid.*

festschrift, Festschrift *n., pl.* **festschrifts, festschriften** a collection of scholarly writings by several authors put together in honor of someone or as a memorial: *Donna contributed a small piece to the festschrift honoring Professor Ofuatey-Kodjoe on his retirement.* See also **florilegium**.

fetid *adj.* foul and smelly: *They trod carefully, trying to keep clear of the fetid muck at the edge of the swamp.*

fey *adj.* strange in a whimsical, eccentric, or otherworldly way: *The success I was having, which I at-*

tributed largely to pure luck, was making me feel quite fey. ∗ The young woman has a fey manner and a mischievous smile.

filial   *adj.* appropriate for or having to do with a son or daughter: *filial respect*

filigree   *v.* to ornament jewelry with fine, lacelike metalwork: *a filigreed pendant* ∗ *(fig.) a guest list filigreed with the names of movie and rock stars*

film noir   *n.* a motion picture of the genre that features an urban setting and a cynical or fatalistic theme, often dealing with corruption or crime, made especially in the 1940s and 1950s: *The movie is a modern film noir.*

fin de siècle, fin-de-siècle   *phrase* relating to Western society and culture at the end of the nineteenth century, or the end of the nineteenth century: *fin-de-siècle materialism* ∗ *The setting of the novel is fin de siècle Vienna.*

finical   *adj.* requiring care, precision, and attention to detail; finicky: *Computers are frustratingly finical machines, but we all continue to use them.*

flagrant   see **blatant/flagrant** at B Confusables

flail   see at F Confusables

flair   see at F Confusables

flare see **flair/flare** at F CONFUSABLES

flatulence see **afflatus/flatulence** at A CONFUSABLES

flaunt see at F CONFUSABLES

flay see **flail/flay** at F CONFUSABLES

flocculent *adj.* like or covered with wool-like tufts or clumps: *He rolled out of bed, his hair a flocculent, ill-behaved crown.*

florescence *n.* the condition of being fully developed or at the height of influence or activity: *Eliot thought the sonnet was a dead form only a few years before it reached a new florescence in the hands of Auden, Frost, Cummings, and others.*

floribunda *n.* a type of rose bush with large flowers, or any showy or flowery display: *She did not play Chopin with the endless trills and insipid floribunda that were popular at the time.*

florilegium *n., pl.* **florilegia** a collection of writings; an anthology: *It's a florilegium about New York City including pieces from the founding of New Amsterdam through the twentieth century.* See also **festschrift**.

flotsam see at F CONFUSABLES

flounder see at F CONFUSABLES

flout see **flaunt/flout** at F CONFUSABLES

folio   *n.* a sheet of paper folded in half to make two leaves or four pages, or a book with large pages, or a page number printed in a book: *a folio edition of Shakespeare's sonnets* * *In the final steps of production, a proofreader will check that the folios are consecutive.* See also **octavo**, **quarto**, **quire**.

Book Words 1:
Words Describing Paper and Printing

Books about words can rarely resist words about books, and this one makes no exception. Many of the terms here are obscure in modern publishing circles, although knowing when to use *recto* and *verso* is one way of showing you have some knowledge of how books are made.

codex   *n.* an ancient manuscript comprised of a number of pages, usually a quire, folded or sewn together, or a manuscript volume of an ancient text.

fascicle   *n.* a bundle, especially the gathered papers of a small piece of writing, which combined with other writings forms a larger work; a section of a book published as a separate piece, or a book in a set published as a separate volume.

folio   *n.* a sheet of paper folded in half to make two leaves or four pages, or a book with large pages, or a page number printed in a book.

incunabula *pl. n.* early printed books made before the invention of movable type.

    incunabular *adj.* having to do with such books.

octavo *n.* a sheet of paper folded three times to make eight leaves or sixteen pages, or a book with small pages.

palimpsest *n.* a reused writing surface, such as parchment, that contains an erased text which can still be discerned beneath the writing of newer text.

quarto *n.* a sheet of paper folded two times to make four leaves or eight pages, or a book with pages of medium size.

quire *n.* a set of twenty-four pieces of paper of the same size and weight; a twentieth of a ream.

recto *n.* the page of a manuscript meant to be read first, or a right-hand page in a book.

verso *n.* the page of a manuscript meant to be read second, or a left-hand page in a book.

foolscap *n.* paper for writing or printing, especially legal-size, lined, yellow paper: *She drew the diagram on a piece of foolscap.* ∗ *a pad of foolscap*

forbear *v. past* **forbore** or **forbear**, *past participle* **forborne** to stop yourself from saying or doing something you would like to do; to refrain from: *"What's that?" asked James. Malcolm and I forbore to reply.* Grammar: The past and past participle are formed in the same way as those of the verb *bear*, "to give birth to a child." See at F CONFUSABLES.

forebear see **forbear/forebear** at F CONFUSABLES

forte *n.* a person's particular talent or skill: *Dancing is not my forte.* Compare **métier**.

fortunate/fortuitous see at F CONFUSABLES

fractal *n.* an irregular curve or other shape that is regularly repeated, or a repeated breaking or disrupting: *The random fractals of social disintegration could be noted throughout the country at the time.*

fractious *adj.* irritable and unruly: *His fractious comments only served to exacerbate an already tense situation.*
  fractiousness *n. Another financial setback has increased fractiousness and caused disagreements among the partners.*

frangible *adj.* able to be broken; fragile: *The surface looked quite solid but proved to be surprisingly frangible.*

freshet *n.* a large, often uncontrolled flow of water, especially an overflow of a river or stream caused by melting snow or heavy rain: *A freshet ran across the trail from the adjoining creek, blocking their path.*

frisson *n.* a sudden sensation, such as a chill or shudder, caused by an emotion: *The haunted house provided surprise, fear, disgust, and the occasional frisson of absolute terror—the kids loved it.*

frustum *n.* a cone-shaped object that is flat on the top, as though the point had been cut off: *Elephants can be taught to climb onto a frustum and stand on two legs.*

fugacious *adj.* **1** lasting only a short time, or quickly disappearing: *These fugacious flowers are among the most highly prized species.* Synonym: **evanescent** **2** disappearing or dropping off before their usual time: *The drought has given us fugacious brown leaves in the middle of summer.*

fulminate *v.* to verbally denounce or condemn, often by shouting: *I can't work with a paranoid constantly fulminating about plots and undermining incompetents.*

fulsome *adj.* abundant to the point of being excessive, especially in a way that is embarrassing or revolting: *I can sit through almost anything, but I found her fulsome praise to be stomach-turning and completely beyond my tolerance levels.* See at F CONFUSABLES. Synonym: **effusive**.

funambulist   *n.* a tightrope walker: *The featured circus artists are an aerialist and a funambulist.*

fungible   *adj.* tradable, exchangeable, or interchangeable: *Fame is not a fungible commodity— different celebrities represent very different things to the public.*
    fungibility   *n. The fungibility of basic commodities is the basic quality that allows social groups to trade with others.*

funicular   *n.* a steeply inclined railway using a cable to pull the cars up the slope and lower them back down: *In Barcelona, we took the funicular up Montjuic to go to the amusement park.*

furbelow   *n.* a ruffle or flounce: *It was one of those B&Bs decked out in Victorian frills and furbelows.*

further   see **farther/further** at F Confusables

G

gaseous/gassy *Gaseous* means existing as a gas (*hydrogen in its gaseous state*); *gassy* means containing gas (*That chili made me pretty gassy.*).

gel/jell see **jell/gel** at J CONFUSABLES

genuine/authentic A *genuine* item is verifiably what it is supposed to be (*genuine diamonds*); an *authentic* item is historically accurate, although it may not be the original (*furniture with authentic period details*).

glance/glimpse As nouns, both words mean a quick look; as a verb, *glance* means to take a quick look (*glance out the window*), while *glimpse* means to see quickly (*I glimpsed Santa coming into the room.*) or to see incompletely (*to glimpse her naked body*).

gourmet/gourmand A *gourmet* is one who is knowledgeable of and enjoys good food and wine (*You need to be a real gourmet to serve as a restaurant critic.*); a *gourmand* is one who enjoys good food and drink, but may not know a lot about them (*The gourmand's motto is, I know what I like.*) See **epicure/gastronome/gourmet** at E CONFUSABLES

---

galumph *v.* to move in a clumsy, awkward, slow-footed way: *He came galumphing across the stage, raising gales of laughter before he'd even opened his mouth.*

gambol *v.* to frolic happily: *In their latest production of* A Midsummer Night's Dream, *there's just too much gamboling about the woods, and nowhere near enough concern taken with the text.*

garrulous *adj.* wordy; talkative, especially about unimportant things: *He hasn't talked about his plans for retirement, but then he isn't the garrulous type.*
    garrulousness *n. Paul's cheerful garrulousness makes him fun to be with.*
    Synonyms: **loquacious, voluble**.

gaseous/gassy see at G CONFUSABLES

gastronome see **epicure/gastronome/gourmet** at E CONFUSABLES

gaucherie *n.* an expression or act that is awkward and crude or lacks grace: *His writing is sophomoric, displaying the enthusiasms and gaucheries of an adolescent perspective.*

gel see **jell/gel** at J CONFUSABLES

gelid *adj.* icy cold: *Almost unbearably hot during the day, when night fell it turned gelid and we huddled close together in an effort to stay warm enough to sleep.*

genuflect *v.* to bend the knee, usually as sign of religious devotion: *He paused for a moment, gazing around the church, then genuflected at the altar.*

genuine see at G CONFUSABLES

geomancy *n.* the art or ability of telling the future by means of lines and figures or by geographic features: *He uses geomancy and feng shui, two ancient earth sciences, to explore the secrets locked in the earth.*

georgic, georgical *adj.* having to do with agriculture or rural life: *Having spent her entire life as a city girl, Tyler was ill-prepared for the georgic life.*
    georgic *n.* a poem about farming or rural life: *She wrote paeans to nature's majesty and georgics extolling the virtues of tilling the soil.*

Waxing Poetic

Reference books won't make
you rich as Croesus
and it's hard to rhyme with *diaeresis*
but poetry offers linguistic filigree
that should keep you from wanting
to write its *elegy*.

anapest   *n.* in poetry, a metrical foot consisting of two short or unstressed syllables followed by a single long or stressed syllable.

dactyl   *n.* a metrical foot in a poem which has one long syllable and two short ones, or one stressed syllable and two unstressed ones.

diaeresis   *n.* a break in a line of poetry that happens when the end of a word and the end of a metric foot coincide.

elegy   *n.* a song or poem with a sad, contemplating tone, especially one suitable or written for the dead.

georgic   *n.* a poem about farming or rural life.

roundelay   *n.* a song or poem with a regular refrain or repeated phrase.

trochee   *n.* a metrical foot in a poem which has one long syllable followed by a short one, or one stressed syllable followed by an unstressed one.

geostationary *adj.* of or having to do with a satellite that travels around the earth's equator at a fixed height and at a speed matching that of the earth's rotation, maintaining a constant relation to points on the earth: *Gigantic geostationary satellites orbit 25,700 miles above earth.*

glance see at G Confusables

glib *adj.* smooth, offhand, and usually insincere: *That guy on the phone was the epitome of the glib, fast-talking salesman—I could hardly get a "no" in edgewise.*
    glibly *adv. She glibly agrees to your plans then goes and does something else every time!*

glimpse see **glance/glimpse** at G Confusables

gourmand *n.* someone who greatly enjoys good food and drink, often to excess: *Michael is what you would call a real gourmand—-he likes nothing better than good food and wine, and the more there is, the better he likes it.* People sometimes use gourmand instead of *gourmet,* meaning a person who is knowledgeable about food without the implication of eating to excess. See **gourmet/gourmand** at G Confusables.

gourmet *n.* someone who is very knowledgeable about and greatly enjoys good food: *He was the kind of guy who could detail his last encounter with a black truffle in loving detail, a real gourmet.* See at G CONFUSABLES. See **epicure/gastronome/gourmet** at E CONFUSABLES. Compare **gourmand**.

gratuitous   *adj.* done without reason or need: *Gratuitous violence is such a mainstay of Hollywood action films that its removal would leave gaping holes in most movies.*

gravamen   *n., pl.* **gravamens** or **gravamina** the part of a charge or an accusation against someone in a court of law that is the most substantial: *The gravamen of the government's case against the trash haulers is their ties to organized crime.*

greaves   *n.* armor worn on the lower legs: *Her legs are bandaged, swollen, and encased in nasty black greaves.*

gregarious   *adj.* enjoying company; sociable: *On Saturday the park is a gregarious hubbub of people talking and laughing, skating, dancing, and playing music.*

grig   *n.* a bright, lively, and engaging person, especially a young person: *She was nearly bouncing down the sidewalk, a grig just dying to share her news with whatever friend she next encountered.*

grisaille   *n.* a three-dimensional effect obtained in painting by using monochromatic gray patterns: *The oppressive prison transmutes everything, even a chartreuse cloth, into the same bleak grisaille.*

guffaw *n.* a loud, hearty laugh: *You could hear the guffawing in the conference room from down the hall.*

guimpe *n.* a cloth worn by nuns over the neck and shoulders: *Sister Martin wore the old things with the arcane names, the wimple, cincture, and guimpe.*

gullible *adj.* easily fooled or cheated: *The Internet, like most other marketplaces, attracts both dishonest venders and gullible clients.* ∗ *Three years ago I was gullible enough to believe that guy's robbery story—he's still working the same corner with the same story.*

guttural *adj.* low, deep, and strange in sound, as if from the throat: *She didn't answer for a long time, then responded with a guttural grunt, as if the very act of acknowledging the question was asking too much of her.*

H

CONFUSABLES

habitat/environment A *habitat* is the place or type of place in which someone or something lives (*Coyotes' habitat has spread to encompass most of North and Central America.*); an *environment* is the combination of factors that influence or affect someone's or something's life (*I've never really adjusted to the office environment.*).

hail/hale *Hail* is used as a noun meaning frozen balls of precipitation (*hail the size of golf balls*) and a greeting or act of calling (*Give them a hail on the radio.*); it is also a verb in these senses (*It started to hail.*) (*Let's hail a taxi.*), and is used in the phrase *hail-fellow-well-met*; *hale* means healthy (*hale and hearty*) and also has the little-used senses of pull and force to go.

happen/transpire see **transpire/happen** at T
CONFUSABLES

hardy/hearty *Hardy* means strong (*a hardy draft animal*), courageous (*Hardy soldiers led the charge.*), brazen (*Hardy criminals pulled off a daring daylight robbery.*), able to withstand cold (*You'd have to be pretty hardy to swim in the Atlantic in January.*), or able to survive the winter outdoors (*hardy perennials*); *hearty* means warmly cordial (*a hearty greeting*), vigorously healthy (*hearty young people who can work long hours*), unequivocal (*a hearty endorsement*), or filling and nourishing (*a hearty meal*).

historic/historical Both words mean important or famous in history; *historic* applies to people or events that will or have become history (*a historic ball game*); *historical* refers to things that are about history (*historical novels*).

homonym/homograph A *homonym* is a word that sounds the same as another word, and may also be spelled the same, but which has a different meaning (*Be* and *bee* are homonyms.); a *homograph* is a word that is spelled the same as another word but has a different meaning and usually a different pronunciation (*The noun* lead *and the verb* lead *are homographs.*).

hopeful/optimistic If you are *hopeful*, you are desiring a good outcome (*I'm hopeful we can finish the job next week.*) or inspiring hope (*She's a hopeful influence around the hospital.*); if you are *optimistic*, you believe the most positive outcome is likely (*Torre is optimistic about the Yankees' chances this year.*).

hue/hew A *hue* is a pale coloration or a particular gradation of color (*The sky was a yellowish hue.*); to *hew* is to cut or fashion with an ax, knife, or other tool (*Woodford hews furniture from driftwood.*).

hypothetical/possible Something *hypothetical* is based on a premise or assertion (*a hypothetical situation*); something *possible* can be achieved under particular circumstances (*one possible outcome of the meeting*).

---

habitat see at H CONFUSABLES

habitué *n.* a frequent visitor to a particular place; a person who does something frequently: *A real habitué of the laundry can ignore the scream of the spin cycle, the dull drone of the dryer.*

hadal *adj.* having to do with the deepest parts of the ocean, below 20,000 feet (6,000 meters): *The deepest oceanic trenches form the hadal region.* See SEA WORDS at **pelagic**.

Hagiographa *pl. n.* the third of the three parts into which the Old Testament is divided in the Jewish tradition, the first part being the Pentateuch and the second part Prophets: *Both Psalms and the Song of Solomon are included in the Hagiographa.*

hagiography *n.* **1** biographical writing that idolizes or glorifies its subject: *This hagiography, written by the governor's former aide and longtime friend, is informative, if rather one-sided.* **2** a biography describing the lives of saints: *It's a pocket-sized version of Englebert's well-known hagiography,* The Lives of the Saints.

    hagiographer *n. This new work illuminates some aspects of Jefferson's life that earlier hagiographers preferred to gloss over.*

hail/hale see at H CONFUSABLES

hamadryad *n.* a wood nymph in classical mythology who inhabits a particular tree and dies when the tree dies. Compare **dryad**.

Hansard *n.* the official published report of the parliamentary proceedings and debates in a British Commonwealth nation.

The Hansard is eponymously named for Luke Hansard, a nineteenth-century British printer who compiled the verbatim reports of the British Parliament.

---

happen see **transpire/happen** at T CONFUSABLES

haptic   *adj.* relating to the sense of touch: *It's likely that virtual technology will one day offer realistic haptic simulations.*

harangue   *n.* a long and vehement speech: *He ignored the deputy's harangue.* Compare **diatribe**.
 harangue *v. He nags and harangues his staff, never offering a word of praise or even of satisfaction with anyone's work.*

harbinger   *n.* something that foretells of something to come, or someone who comes in advance to announce an arrival: *People have begun to think this hot, dry summer is a harbinger of the posited era of global warming.*

hardy/hearty see at H CONFUSABLES

hegemony   *n.* predominance, or the principal influence on an event or on something's existence: *By 1984, the long-lived O'Malley hegemony over the Dodgers had come to an end.*

heliotrope   *n.* a plant that turns to follow the sun throughout the day: *She turns, keeping her face to the camera like a heliotrope following the sun.*

hemidemisemiquaver   *n. esp. British* a sixty-fourth note

hemophilia   *n.* a medical condition in which the blood clots very slowly so that even a minor injury causes dangerous excessive bleeding: *He was given medication by a Tibetan monk to treat his hemophilia.*

hemophiliac *n. Several members of the czar's family were hemophiliacs.*

hemorrhage *v.* to bleed excessively or uncontrollably: *He was hemorrhaging severely when he was brought to the hospital.*

hemorrhage *n. Alexis died of a massive hemorrhage.*

hemorrhagic *adj. hemorrhagic illnesses*

henotheism *n.* belief in or worship of a single god without denying the existence of others: *He decries what he perceives as the growing henotheism of American culture in which people seem ready to accept all religions as equally true.*

hermetic *adj.* airtight, or unable to be breached: *a hermetic seal* * *She's completely uncommunicative, living in her own little hermetic universe.*

hermetically *adv. He created a whole world in that comic strip, hermetically sealed off, entirely on its own.*

heteronym *n.* one of two or more words that have identical spellings but different meanings and pronunciations, such as *lead* (a metal) and *lead* (to direct or guide)

hew see **hue/hew** at H CONFUSABLES

hidebound   *adj.* stubborn and inflexible: *The hidebound conventions of the Society scared off many of the younger applicants.*

historic/historical see at H CONFUSABLES

histrionic   *adj.* loud and full of wild gestures; overacted: *My mother's histrionic impulses made it almost impossible for her to keep a secret.*
   histrionics   *pl. n.* overacting or overreacting: *You'll have to forgive my son's histrionics—he's been having a very hard day.*

hob   *n.* harm, irritation, mischief, or trouble: *Why would we invite someone to join us if we thought their only goal was to play hob with our project?* Usually used in the phrases *play hob with* or *raise hob with.*

hokum   *n.* nonsense; something trite or irrelevant: *Their act was pure hokum, and I loved every minute of it.* * *You can't believe a word of that hokum that politicians spout.*

homonym/homograph see at H CONFUSABLES

homunculus   *n.* a very short man, or a dwarf: *His little tutor in the intricacies of the game, his chess homunculus, had failed to appear as scheduled.*

hopeful see at H CONFUSABLES

hoplite *n.* a heavily armed foot soldier in ancient Greece: *The block was taken over by the SWAT team—the hoplites of the modern police force.*

horrent *adj.* covered with bristles, or bristling: *The crocheted dragon has a crest of taffeta plates like horrent scallops.*

hubris *n.* arrogance and an inflated sense of self-worth resulting usually from pride: *It was an act of real hubris to start showing people my landscaping before the spring rains started and washed away most of the carefully laid out beds.*

hue see at H CONFUSABLES

hyperbole *n.* exaggeration used for emphasis or to achieve an effect: *Right now we want to lay out all the program's basic features and save the hyperbole for the presentation to the sales staff.*
  hyperbolic *adj. Early in a campaign, only the speeches were hyperbolic, but with the nomination in reach, every public appearance is an exaggerated effort to capture TV time.*

hypothermia *n.* extremely low body temperature: *She'd been out in the cold for too long and was beginning to worry about hypothermia.*

hypothetical see at H CONFUSABLES

I

CONFUSABLES

ibid./op. cit. *Ibid.*, short for *ibidem*, "in the same place," is used in footnotes with a page number to refer to the immediately preceding footnote; *op. cit.* short for *opere citato*, "in the work cited," is used in footnotes with an author's name and a page number as a shorthand reference subsequent to the first citation of a work.

idiot/moron see **moron/idiot** at M CONFUSABLES

idle/idyll *Idle* means inactive (*an idle engine*) or useless (*idle talk*); an *idyll* is a peaceful, contented rural experience (*Michael and David's place in Hankin offers a relaxing idyll.*)

illicit/illegal An *illicit* act is one prohibited by law or custom (*an illicit sexual liaison*); an *ille-*

gal act is prohibited only by law (*It's illegal to yell "fire" in a crowded theater.*).

illusive/elusive see **elusive/illusive** at E CONFUS-ABLES

imaginary/imaginative If something is *imaginary* it exists only in the imagination (*imaginary friends*); if something is *imaginative*, it was created using imagination (*an imaginative story*).

immigrate/emigrate see **emigrate/immigrate** at E CONFUSABLES

imminent/eminent see **eminent/imminent** at E CONFUSABLES

immoral/amoral see **amoral/immoral** at A CONFUSABLES

immovable/irremovable Something that is *immovable* is physically impossible to move (*the immovable mountains*); something *irremovable* cannot be taken away or removed (*Presidents think of themselves as irremovable until impeachment hearings begin.*).

impugn/malign see **malign/impugn** at M CONFUSABLES

impugn/oppugn see **oppugn/impugn** at O CONFUSABLES

inapt/inept *Inapt* means unsuitable or inappropriate (*an inapt remark*); *inept* means incompetent (*An inept bookkeeper can be disastrous for a small company.*); each of these words is sometimes used as a synonym for the other.

inartistic/unartistic see **unartistic/inartistic** at U CONFUSABLES

inculcate/indoctrinate To *inculcate* is to teach by forceful repetition (*Madame LeClerc tried to inculcate the conjugations of irregular French verbs.*); to *indoctrinate* is to brainwash (*Hitler Youth were indoctrinated to believe Germans were superior.*).

infuse/imbue Both words mean to permeate; *infuse* is used when aspirations, ideas, or principles are involved (*infuse with a sense of duty*) or when tea is being made (*infuse the water with cinnamon*); *imbue* is used when colors are being added (*paintings imbued with the subtle colors of the forest*); both words can be used to suggest that a text or other work is permeated with something.

insightful/perceptive *Insightful* means characterized by intuitive understanding and describes the ability to understand the inner nature of something (*She made some insightful comments about the nature of the creative process.*); *perceptive* means characterized by the ability to clearly see and understand and describes the external aspects of something (*She made a perceptive comment about my apparent discomfort.*).

insinuate/imply To *insinuate* means to work in subtly and sneakily (*Are you insinuating that I'm stupid?*); to *imply* means to state indirectly, though not necessarily sneakily (*His actions imply a love of animals.*).

intra-/inter- *Intra-* combines with nouns to add the meaning within, inside of, or between the layers of (*an intrasquad workout * intramuscular injections*); *inter-* combines with nouns to add the meaning between (*intercity travel * interpersonal relations*)

invidious/insidious *Invidious* means promoting resentment or unrest (*She made some invidious remarks about how "those people" behave.*); *insidious* means sneakily attractive (*insidious advertisements*) or slowly affecting (*the insidious effects of acid rain*).

invoke/evoke see **evoke/invoke** at E Confus-
ABLES

---

ibid. see at I Confusables

ichor *n.* a thin, watery, acrid discharge from a wound or ulcer
(see note next page)

In classical mythology, ichor is the fluid that runs through the veins of the gods instead of blood.

ichthyology   *n.* the scientific study of fish: *There aren't many schools where you can major in ichthyology and minor in African literature.* See also **saurian**.

   ichthyologist   *n. In amongst the competitors in the deep-sea fishing rodeo was a U Mass ichthyologist looking to acquire fish skeletons of species he hadn't yet collected.*

iconography   *n.* an image that is a symbolic representation of something: *Nast's famous image of Santa pulled together various elements of the Santa iconography.*

   iconographic, **iconographical**   *adj. The opening number employed the iconographic ice skating reference to Hans Christian Andersen in the hands-behind-the-back, side-to-side glide of the choreography.*

ideogram, ideograph   *n.* a written symbol representing a thing, idea, or concept: *Similar ideograms, such as a cigarette in a red circle with a diagonal through it to indicate no smoking is allowed, are used in many countries to provide warnings and information.* Synonym: **logogram**.

idiot   see **moron/idiot** at M Confusables

idle see at I Confusables

idolatry *n.* **1** the worship of statues or other representations of religious figures, or worship of the gods of polytheistic religions: *People don't worship the statue itself, but what it represents, so you can't say it's idolatry!* **2** extreme devotion to someone or something: *Some superstars enjoy the idolatry, and others hate it.*

idyll see **idle/idyll** at I Confusables

idyllic *adj.* ideal, serene, or perfect in a romantic or carefree way: *The game of baseball bears the idyllic imprint of youth and serves as a mirror of American character, a creator of its heroes.*

ilk *n.* a type, kind, group, class, or family: *The governor and his ilk lower taxes while saddling government with increased debt.* Usually used negatively.

illegal see **illicit/illegal** at I Confusables

illicit see at I Confusables

illimitable *adj.* without limit: *Contemplating life after college, the possibilities for the future were illimitable—and rather scary.* * *The uses of this programming language would seem illimitable within the framework of current technology.*

illusive see **elusive/illusive** at E Confusables

imaginary/imaginative see at I CONFUSABLES

imbue *v.* to fill, saturate, or permeate: *I try to imbue the outline with a graceful freedom as I draw.* See **infuse/imbue** at I CONFUSABLES

immanent *adj.* having, being, or remaining in someone or something: *My own immanent sense of dread prevented me from having a good time.*
 immanence, immanency *n.* the state of being within: *Even though he was dead, I felt the immanence of his presence.*

immemorial *adj.* extending back in time to before record or memory: *Their ancestors migrated here in the immemorial past. * Our people have fished these waters since time immemorial.* Used most often in the phrases *since time immemorial* and *from time immemorial.*

immigrate see **emigrate/immigrate** at E CONFUSABLES

imminent see **eminent/imminent** at E CONFUSABLES

immiscible *adj.* incapable of being blended together or mixed with another substance: *The fat is immiscible in the broth and will rise to the top where it can be skimmed off.*

immoral see **amoral/immoral** at A CONFUSABLES

immovable see at I CONFUSABLES

immure *v.* to enclose, imprison, or shut in: *Betty seems immured in disappointment.*

immutable *adj.* unchanging; not subject to change: *How you schedule your time is up to you; the only immutable rule is the project must be finished on time.* ∗ *Taxonomies are not immutable: whether you see astrophysics as a part of physics, or a part of astronomy, or both depends on the theory of classification you use.*
    immutably *adv. Izzy was immutably uncommunicative with strangers.*
    immutability *n. The seasons change, and that they change is part of the immutability of nature.*

impalpable *adj.* not able to be understood by touch; intangible: *The value of my musical education is impalpable but far reaching.* ∗ *I was suddenly gripped by impalpable dread.* Antonym: **palpable**.
    impalpably *adv. The theory seemed to me impalpably difficult to grasp.*

impeccable *adj.* flawless, perfect: *His timing was impeccable.*

impercipient *adj.* without perception: *His reactions seemed impercipient, as though he'd never heard about the tragedy.*

imperious *adj.* superior in attitude, because of social rank or an overly high opinion of oneself:

He waved her away with an imperious flip of his hand.

imperiously   *adv. He gazed imperiously out on the crowd, thinking of how every occupied seat meant more money in his pocket.*

imperium   *n., pl.* **imperia, imperiums 1** a sphere of power, control, or monopoly: *Now we will have to choose a company to supply our gas and electricity, just as we had to choose a telephone company after the forced demise of the AT&T imperium.* **2** a superpower: *For much of the second half of the twentieth century, world politics was dominated by the twin imperia of the United States and the Soviet Union.*

impetus   *n., pl.* **impetuses** a moving force; an impulse or incentive: *Steve Jobs once again seems to be the impetus propelling Apple toward innovative design and new customers.*

implacable   *adj.* not able to be appeased: *Her implacable attitude could not be overcome—she was displeased and would stay that way.*

implacably   *adv. He implacably insisted he would see the mayor, regardless of not having an appointment.*

imply see **insinuate/imply** at I Confusables

importunate   *adj.* persistent and annoying: *I'm bothered by these importunate memories of my high-school years.*

importune *v.* to beg earnestly for something or to make persistent requests; annoy: *She tried to get him to talk to his father, but her importuning was in vain.* * *She importunes on behalf of her client; that's her job.*

 importuning *adj. You can get rid of these importuning telephone solicitors by asking to be placed on their do-not-call list.*

impost *n.* **1** a tax or levy: *A more practical solution would be to house both teams in a single stadium, which would cut the enormous impost on the city in half.* **2** the part of a building, such as a block or capital, where an arch begins: *The decorative sculpture on the facing of the impost is most unusual.*

imprecate *v.* to curse: *Children today feel they can imprecate their teachers or spit at an umpire without fear of retribution.*

 imprecation *n. As he strode to the podium, imprecations were hurled at him by the unruly crowd.*

improvident *adj.* lacking foresight, or without thought for future needs: *Selling your stock at this time would be improvident.*

impudent *adj.* brazenly disrespectful or contemptuous of others: *Al's superiors branded him an impudent troublemaker, someone who should be eased out of the organization at the first opportunity.*

impugn see **malign/impugn** at M Confusables; see **oppugn/impugn** at O Confusables

impunity   *n.* immunity or exemption from punishment, harm, or deleterious consequences: *It was once so wild here that people were smoking pot with impunity.*

in extremis *phrase* in an extreme circumstance, or at the point of death: *The idea behind a nuclear deterrent is to "deter" the other guy from using nukes, and use ours only in extremis.* ∗ *He was found lying on the floor, in extremis, and may not survive.*

in situ *phrase* in the original place or position; localized: *The artifacts have been left in situ, but the site can be viewed during scheduled underground tours.*

inamorata   *n.* the woman whom someone loves, or the woman who is one's lover: *He watched as his inamorata slowly removed her clothes.*

inamorato   *n.* the man whom someone loves, or the man who is one's lover: *She was relieved when she finally saw her inamorato coming off the plane.*

inapt see at I Confusables

inarticulacy   *n.* the state or quality of being inarticulate: *Much has been written and said about the inarticulacy of painters.*

inartistic see **unartistic/inartistic** at U CONFUSABLES

inauspicious *adj.* unfavorable; of a bad or evil omen: *The storm last night was an inauspicious start to our camping trip.* Compare **ominous**; **portentous.**

incipient *adj.* in the earliest stage; beginning to come into existence: *We didn't realize his styles portended an incipient revolution in men's fashion.*

incommensurable *adj.* not comparable by the same measure or standard, or not meriting comparison: *These authors' works are incommensurable.* Antonym: **commensurable**.

incommensurate *adj.* not adequate, or not equal to something else: *The school received an incommensurate supply of examination booklets.* Antonym: **commensurate**.

incongruous *adj.* out of place, not suitable or compatible, or not in character: *Although I knew of his conversion from off-the-wall yippie to conservative entrepreneur, I still found it incongruous for him to be ringing the bell to open the day's trading on Wall Street.*
    incongruity *n. The incongruity of hiring convicted felons to provide security seems to have gone unnoticed by managers concerned only with cutting costs.*

incredulous   *adj.* **1** feeling or expressing disbelief: *We laughed and talked and kissed and talked some more, incredulous that this evening had somehow come to exist.* **2** incredible: *I had this incredulous feeling of relief when I finished the project.*

  incredulously   *adv. She put her head back and laughed incredulously at her good fortune.*

incubus   *n., pl.* **incubi** a demon or evil spirit, or any oppressive or nightmarish force: *She saw him now not just as a frightening man, but as an ancient, unyielding force that stood between her and her destiny, as an incubus who kept pressing her down.* Compare **succubus**.

> In medieval times, an incubus was thought to be a devil in the form of a man who had sex with a sleeping woman.

inculcate see at I CONFUSABLES

inculpate   *v.* to incriminate or show the guilt of: *It's hard to imagine that a mother would be willing to give testimony that might inculpate her own daughter.*

incunabula   *pl. n.* early printed books made before the invention of movable type: *The museum owns several of these rare incunabula.* The singular, **incunabulum**, is less used.

incunabular   *adj. The Morgan Library owns one of the world's foremost incunabular collections.*

incursion   *n.* a sudden, aggressive, or undesirable entrance, especially a raid or invasion: *a border incursion * An incursion through a break in the sea wall at the north end of the island caused widespread flooding.*

indefatigable   *adj.* untiring: *These men and women are being honored for their indefatigable efforts on behalf of those left homeless by the hurricane.*

indict   *v.* to accuse someone of a crime, especially in order to hold a trial in a court of law: *I felt I'd been indicted without a fair hearing.*

indigenous   *adj.* originating in or belonging to a particular place: *The potato, tomato, and pepper, as well as chocolate and vanilla, are indigenous to the Americas. * indigenous architecture*

indite   *v.* to express, describe, or compose: *Some hosts take extraordinary pains in composing their words and indite truly elegant introductions.*

indoctrinate see **inculcate/indoctrinate** at I CONFU-SABLES

indolence   *n.* laziness; sloth: *Even for a teenager, his indolence is remarkable.*
   indolent   *adj. Go wake up your indolent brother.*

ineffable   *adj.* unable to be expressed in words, because of being too wonderful, too horrible, or taboo: *The locker room celebrations were marked with the ineffable joy of a championship that was hard won. * The ineffable horror of a child's death brings unmitigated guilt to everyone who knew that child, even though—or perhaps, because—there was nothing they could have done to change the outcome.*

   ineffably   *adv.* indescribably or unspeakably: *The children's funeral was an ineffably sad occasion.*

ineluctable   *adj.* certain to come to pass; inevitable: *For years we lived in the countryside, but that countryside ultimately succumbed to the ineluctable forces of development and sprawl. * The ineluctable call of destiny led her to this career.*

   ineluctably   *adv. In the late fifties the Soviet Union seemed ineluctably on course to overtake the U.S. economically and militarily.*

inept see **inapt/inept** at I Confusables

inertia   *n.* the property of matter that keeps an object still if it is at rest or moving if it is in motion, unless some force acts upon it; more broadly, the tendency of a person or thing to remain still, not exert itself, and not change unless forced to: *She*

*feels trapped and is hoping to find the path of action
that will let her escape—-she could tolerate success
or failure, but not inertia.*

inexorably *adv.* unrelentingly, unremittingly: *He
populates his novels with men and women who are
inexorably stylish and always stay out late.*
   inexorable *adj. the inexorable march of time*

infamous *adj.* disreputable and widely known;
notorious: *An infamous womanizer and lush, he
ultimately found himself out of luck and out of
work.*
   infamously *adv. Brooklynites still resent the man
who infamously abducted the Dodgers and took
them to California.*

infuse see at I CONFUSABLES

ingenuous *adj.* candid and sincere, straightforward: *The man struck me as ingenuous and likable.*
   ingenuousness *n. I was struck by the ingenuousness of her performance.*

inhere *v.* to be inherent in or fundamentally be-
long to something: *the advantages that inhere to a
healthy lifestyle*

inimical *adj.* having a harmful effect: *The design
for the building is one I might like in some other
setting, but it is inimical to this historic district.*

inimitable *adj.* matchless; not possible to imitate: *She dances Balanchine's choreography with inimitable style and grace.*

    inimitability, inimitableness *n. Several exhibited pieces may be by other artists, leaving one to wonder if there is true inimitability in this Old Master's style.*

iniquity *n.* injustice, or lack of fairness: *It wasn't only the iniquity of the fire department's promotion system but also its apparent illegality that led him to sue.*

inselberg *n.* a mountain that stands alone; monadnock.

insentient *adj.* without sensation or consciousness: *I would prefer sentient mortality to insentient immortality.*

insidious *adj.* intended to entrap or deceive; subtly harmful or undermining: *This intentional misrepresentation of the facts is an insidious attempt to undermine my authority.* See **invidious/insidious** at I Confusables.

insightful see at I Confusables

insinuate see at I Confusables

insouciant *adj.* carefree and unconcerned: *I'm jealous of his insouciant ease with strangers.*

    insouciance *n. Some people find his insouciance off-putting, but I find it refreshing.* ∗ *We created* *an atmosphere where our guests can dine in a happy insouciance.*

intaglio   *n.* a picture or design incised or etched into a surface, or an engraved plate for printing: *The rough intaglios were filled with hot metal, and the cooled rectangles were recast into curved plates for the rotary cylinders of the printing presses.*

integument, tegument   *n.* a layer or covering like a skin: *She'd been out riding all afternoon, and a thin integument of grit covered her body like a sheath.*

inter- see **intra-/inter-** at I Confusables

inter alia   *phrase* among other things: *The composer worked as, inter alia, a cab driver before his success in Amsterdam and New York.*

internecine   *adj.* relating to struggle within an organization, group, or territory: *The family was notorious for its internecine rivalries.*

interpolate   *v.* to insert or place additional words in the middle of a text or in discourse: *Shakespeare would interpolate inadvertent asides to give his actors more natural-sounding dialogue.*

interregnum   *n., pl.* **interregnums, interregna** a period of time when the usual authority, rules, or attitudes do not apply, especially a time between rulers or governments; an interruption in continuity: *In* *what was an all-too-brief interregnum, the political leaders of both parties gave up their partisan posturing and worked toward compromise.*

intifada, intifadeh   *n.* a rebellion, specifically the rebellion of Palestinians against the Israeli military's occupation of territory along the west bank of the Jordan River and in the Gaza Strip: *The onset of spring brings an upsurge in animal spirits, an exultant intifada of our animal nature.*

intimate   *v.* to make something known in an indirect way; to hint at or imply: *The garden's shadowed arbors and close lanes seemed to intimate tension and despair.* ∗ *They are old friends, but they've intimated that romance has suddenly bloomed.*

intra- see at I CONFUSABLES

intractable   *adj.* unmanageable or untreatable, or stubborn and unwilling to accept change or direction: *She presents it as some sort of intractable problem, but if she'd just buckle down and work on it I'm sure she could solve it in no time.* ∗ *I suggested it might be a good idea to see a doctor, but he was intractable in his refusal to seek medical care.*
   intractably   *adj. They are both intractably obstinate.*
   intractability, intractableness   *n.* the quality of being unworkable or unmanageable: *The intractability of the novelist's material has kept her from finishing the book.*

intransigent *adj.* inflexible and unwilling to compromise: *The negotiators had taken an intransigent position.*

　intransigent *n.* a person, especially a politician, who is unwilling to compromise or agree with others: *His reputation as an intransigent hurt his chances for a leadership position in the party.*

　intransigence *n.* unwillingness to compromise or to accept something: *There was a note of intransigence in his voice.*

　intransigently *adv.* *You can't work with someone who so intransigently refuses to compromise.*

invective *n.* a vehement insult, denunciation, or accusation: *The minister was widely criticized for his invective regarding a popular children's TV show.* * *She had a sailor's command of invective, but beneath the hard exterior was a pussycat.*

inveigh *v.* to complain loudly or object to strongly: *In the Roaring Twenties, temperance supporters continually inveighed against the use of alcohol.*

inveigle *v.* to coax or win someone over: *She inveigled us into going out line dancing on Saturday.*

invidious *adj.* causing or intending to cause resentment or ill will; intentionally annoying: *Her invidious comments were intended to anger the crowd.* See at I CONFUSABLES.

invoke see **evoke/invoke** at E CONFUSABLES

irascible *adj.* **1** resulting from anger: *The attempt at negotiation ended in an irascible standoff instead of an agreement.* **2** irritable and easily angered: *He was, by turns, incredibly patient and disturbingly irascible, and you never knew which character would appear.* ∗ *my irascible neighbor*

   irascibility, irascibleness *n. The senator's irascibility was really just posturing, meant to prove a point.*

iridescent *adj.* having lustrous colors: *Fog descended on the beach in an iridescent haze.*

irreal *adj.* unreal: *When we left the ball, our host brought us to a nightclub we couldn't have gotten into on our own, and seeing the princess and her party a few tables over, I decided it might be quite irreal, but I was going to enjoy it.*

irremovable see **immovable/irremovable** at I CON-FUSABLES

irrespective of *prep.* without consideration of or regard for: *Bergman always felt that, irrespective of everything, the performance must go on.*

irreverent *adj.* not showing the proper respect toward authority: *Lou could be obscenely irreverent, especially to bureaucrats who wanted him to conform to regulations.*

irruption *n.* an intrusion into something; an invasion: *The cell phone has caused an irruption of once private communications into public space.*

isonomous, isonomic *adj.* having equality in political rights: *The desire for isonomous status for African Americans drove the civil rights efforts of the sixties.*

J

CONFUSABLES

jell/gel *Jell* is a verb meaning to congeal (*Wait for the pudding to jell.*); *gel* is a noun, short for *gelatin* and meaning a jelly made from animal protein or a thin colored sheet placed over lights.

jetsam/flotsam see **flotsam/jetsam** at F CONFUSABLES

Jacobin *n.* **1** a radical or member of an extremist group: *The Jacobins of PETA have no qualms about attacking humans in the defense of animals.* **2** a radical republican during the French Revolution **3** a Dominican friar or monk

jejune *adj.* dull, uninteresting, and immature or childish: *Whenever we see him, he inflicts more of his terribly jejune stories on us.*

jell see at J CONFUSABLES

jeremiad *n.* a lengthy complaint, or an exhortation of warning: *There is little to lift you from doom and gloom in this jeremiad on the plunder of the country's hoard of natural resources.*

jetsam see **flotsam/jetsam** at F CONFUSABLES

jocund *adj.* displaying gaiety, high spirits, and a lively, happy attitude: *After a week on my own, I longed for the jocund fellowship I had enjoyed with my buddies back home.*

joie de vivre *phrase* enjoyment of life: *It seems like, whatever he does, he does it with an infectious joie de vivre.*

judder *v.* to wiggle and shake: *His headlights juddered as he drove over the log bridge.*

jugate *adj.* being arranged in pairs: *The jugate cylinders push the crankshaft in turns, keeping it rotating smoothly.*

junket *n.* a trip, especially one paid for by public funds or by a corporate sponsor: *Eventually, Frank tired of traveling to Japan to see the latest electronics innovation, and turned down most of the junkets that were offered to him.*
    junket *v. He went to Russia ostensibly to research the book, but he appears to have been jun-*

keting at his publisher's expense, and has little to show for it.

jurisprudence *n.* the philosophy and science of law, or a particular area of law: *His jurisprudence reflects liberal humanist principles.* * *civil jurisprudence*

jus sanguinis *n.* the right of a child to citizenship based on the parents' citizenship

jus soli *n.* the right of a child to citizenship based on his or her place of birth

juxtaposition *n.* placement of things together, allowing them to be compared and contrasted: *The three works are displayed together in a smaller gallery, where their juxtaposition clearly reveals their thematic similarities.*

K

CONFUSABLES

karat/carat/caret see **carat/karat/caret** at C CONFUSABLES

kith/kin *Kith* are nearby neighbors and friends; *kin* are relatives; the phrase *kith and kin* pertains to friends and relatives.

---

kabala, kabbala, kabbalah, cabala, cabbala, cabbalah *n.* a mystical Jewish system of beliefs which holds that the Scriptures are a coded text and that the universe came into being by radiating from God: *He is a famous historian of the kabbala.*

kahuna *n.* a Hawaiian medicine man or witch doctor: *She went to some kahuna for help with her husband's impotence.*

karat see **carat/karat/caret** at C CONFUSABLES

katabatic *adj.* having to do with a wind produced by a cold air mass moving down the slope of a mountain or glacier: *Although well below the snow line, the village is cooled by katabatic winds from the surrounding mountains.*

kelpie *n.* a creature, usually in the shape of a horse, that in Scottish folklore causes travelers to drown: *Some villagers still swear there are kelpies living near those lochs.*

kerfuffle *n.* confusion or a disturbance: *On the porch, a kerfuffle over when and why a president could be impeached involved half the guests.*

kine *n.* an archaic plural of *cow*: *From over the rise, we could hear the gentle lowing of kine.* A rare word in that it has no letters in common with its singular form.

kith/kin see at K CONFUSABLES

kiva *n.* a round structure built by Pueblo Indians that is partly underground and was probably used for various ceremonial functions: *Kivas at Mesa Verde remain an intriguing mystery.*

kleptocracy *n.* government in which greed and corruption are rampant: *Much of Africa has a tradition of kleptocracy that developed under colonial rule.*

knout *n.* a whip used to flog people: *He raised the knout above his head, then paused for the effect it would have on the crowd.*

knout *v. The punishment for such offenses was to be knouted in the town square.*

koan *n.* a puzzle or paradox intended as a subject of Zen meditation: *The headline was a play on the most famous koan, What is the sound of one hand clapping?*

  koanlike *adj. His cryptic answer stayed with me, developing a koanlike quality as I tossed it around in my head.*

koumiss, kumiss *n.* a drink made from fermented horse's milk that originated from central Asian nomads

kouros *n., pl.* **kouroi** a statue, typically made in ancient Greece, of a naked boy or young man standing with his hands by his sides and his left leg coming forward: *Harry would spend hours at the Met enjoying the finely sculpted forms of his favorite kouroi.*

Kyrie, Kyrie eleison *n.* a short prayer said as part of a Christian church service that begins with the words "Lord, have mercy."

L

CONFUSABLES

laudable/laudatory *Laudable* means praise-worthy or deserving praise (*Her heroism is laudable.*); *laudatory* means expressing praise (*The mayor made laudatory comments about her heroism.*).

lectern/podium A *lectern* is a stand that supports a speaker's notes (*He has an annoying habit of tapping on the lectern as he speaks.*); a *podium* is a platform on which a speaker stands (*Come up to the podium if you want to address the group.*).

legation/delegation A *legation* is a diplomatic mission to a foreign county that ranks below an embassy (*the U.S. legation to Mozambique*); a *delegation* is an officially elected or appointed group of representatives (*the New*

York delegation to the Republican national convention).

levee/levy A *levee* is a dike or earthen embankment (*We stood out on the levee, skipping stones and talking.*); a *levy* is a tax (*New levies on cigarettes have been proposed.*).

libel/slander In legal use, *libel* is written, published material that defames and damages another's reputation (*The magazine was convicted of libel.*); *slander* is an oral statement that defames and damages someone's reputation (*He claims the comments slandered him.*).

loath/loathe *Loath*, an adjective, means unwilling (*I'm loath to take on another project like this one.*); *loathe*, a verb, means despise or hate (*I loathe working during vacations.*).

luxuriant/luxurious *Luxuriant* means abundant or rich and varied (*Luxuriant undergrowth surrounds the house*); both *luxurious* and *luxuriant* mean easy and comfortable (*a luxurious life*), expensive and high quality (*a luxuriant Rolls-Royce*), and self-indulgent (*She spent a luxurious hour lolling in the bathtub.*).

---

laager *n.* a defense against attack, or a position from which one can defend oneself: *More and more suburban communities have raised high-tech, high-*

security laagers against the possibility of infiltration by the poor, the unwashed, and the dark-skinned.

labyrinthine, **labyrinthian**   *adj.* winding, intricate, or confusing: *I got lost trying to find my way through the labyrinthine passageways connecting the hospital buildings. * The procedure for applying for the mortgage was unnecessarily labyrinthine.*

laconic   *adj.* using few words; terse: *It was another of the judge's laconic opinions.*

lacrimation   *n.* the act of crying, especially excessively: *The public demands confession, breast-beating, and lacrimation from public figures who have been caught with their pants down.*

lambaste   *v.* to attack physically or verbally in a vigorous way: *I gave up baseball when it became clear the coach would lambaste me in front of my teammates for every minor miscue I made.*

lambent   *adj.* radiant and flickering, or having a bright expression: *Gazing out at the lambent faces of these adorable four year olds filled my heart with joy.*

languor   *n.* weakness and a lack of energy: *Everyone was suffering from a languor brought on by the continuing heat wave.*
   languorous   *adj.* without energy and vitality; sluggish: *We sat under the trees, hoping to escape*

the oppressiveness of another humid, languorous day.

Laodicean   *adj.* indifferent, unconcerned, or lukewarm in matters of religion or politics: *The party's right wing finds the candidate's lack of positions unacceptably Laodicean.*

In the New Testament book of Revelation (3:14–22), the Apostle John is told to address the church in Laodicea about its members' indifference.

Laputan   *adj.* ridiculously impractical or devoted to visionary undertakings while neglecting more useful activities: *She pursues these Laputan schemes and then seems surprised when she doesn't have money to pay the rent.*

In *Gulliver's Travels* by Jonathan Swift, Laputa is a flying island where people devote themselves to impractical, visionary projects.

lascivious   *adj.* lustful, arousing sexual desire or interest: *a lascivious old man* ∗ *Her lascivious gestures were, alas, not meant as an invitation.* Compare **libidinous**.

lassitude   *n.* a feeling of weariness or of being tired and lifeless: *I felt feverish, trapped by this lassitude without any desire to leave my bed.* ∗ *Our family* *took a no-nonsense, pull-your-socks-up attitude toward fecklessness, lassitude, or any similar condition that was brought on by anything less than near-fatal diseases.*

laudable/laudatory see at L CONFUSABLES

lazaretto, lazaret, lazarette *n.* **1** a hospital for patients who have contracted contagious diseases: *The mission also ran a lazaretto and a convalescent building.* **2** a building or ship in which quarantined patients are kept **3** a storage space located between the decks of a ship

lectern see at L CONFUSABLES

legation see at L CONFUSABLES

legerdemain *n.* clever, skillful trickery; sleight of hand: *It was fancy, legal legerdemain that gained the conviction, and there will be an appeal!*

leitmotiv, leitmotif *n.* a recurring theme or pattern: *Delay has been the leitmotiv of the approval process.*

lemma *n., pl.* **lemmas, lemmata 1** a secondary proposition that is used in an argument to demonstrate another proposition: *Not only was it morally indefensible but, as his lemma posited, it would destabilize familes.* **2** a theme or subject shown in a title: *Some scholars are able to describe your theo-*

rem after simply seeing your lemma. **3** a word or phrase as it appears in a glossary

levee/levy see at L Confusables

libel see at L Confusables

libidinous *adj.* filled with lust: *The libidinous hedonism of the late seventies gave way to caution, pragmatism, and fear a decade later.* Compare **lascivious**.

Lilliputian *adj.* very small in size, or trivial: *I feel our contribution has been Lilliputian in comparison to the effort needed.*

In *Gulliver's Travels* by Jonathan Swift, Lilliput is a land where everyone and everything is tiny.

limen *n.* an emotional or psychological threshold or limit: *His constant nagging had surpassed the limen of her tolerance, and she fondled the knife thoughtfully.* See also **liminal**.

liminal *adj.* limited, or marked by limits or boundaries: *We allow the kids some freedom, but it's a liminal sort of freedom, not an absolute license to do as they please.* See also **limen**.

limn *v.* to represent in a drawing or painting, or to draw or paint a picture or outline of someone or something: *The lines of the cartoon experienced a voluptuous thickening when limning the curves of Daisy Mae or Moonbeam McSwine. * She limns the contours of the surface, imbuing them with an extraordinary grace.*

limpet *n.* **1** a mollusk with a cone-shaped shell which adheres to rocks in tidal areas **2** one that clings to someone or something: *These lobbyists are limpets affixing themselves to representatives who show even a hint of being persuaded.* **3** an explosive that magnetically attaches to the hull of a ship

litigious *adj.* prone to initiating, or carrying on, lawsuits: *There is no doubt that ours is a litigious society.*
   litigiousness *n. The litigiousness of the industry has cost billions of dollars.*

litterateur, littérateur *n.* a writer, or a person devoted to studying literature: *The thought that one brave person may have rejected the movie theater and gone home to a chapter of Thomas Pynchon is enough to wet the eyes of the stoniest litterateur.*

littoral *n.* the shore of an ocean, sea, or lake: *The increase in the number of homes built on the littoral means an increased risk of property loss in the event of a hurricane.*

loath/loathe see at L Confusables

locus *n.* place; a position or location: *From my*

locus behind a pillar, I couldn't see half of the stage. ∗ *This hill was the locus of a two-day battle during the Civil War.*

locution   *n.* a way of speaking, or a particular way of phrasing something: *He was uncomfortable with the fact that he was gay, and never referred to his boyfriends as such, preferring the locution "pals."*

lodestone   *n.* **1** something that strongly attracts: *His music is his lodestone.* **2** a variety of the mineral magnetite that has magnetic properties

logo- *prefix* word, or speech: *Mike is becoming a real logophile—he just loves words.* ∗ *She goes on and on like a regular logomaniac, talking from the time she wakes up till she falls asleep at night.*

logogram, logograph   *n.* a written symbol or sign that represents a word: *While we are wedded to our alphabet, there is nothing to make it intrinsically superior to Chinese logograms.* Synonym: **ideogram**.

logograph   *n.* See at **logogram**.

longueur   *n.* a dull section of a literary or artistic work: *While it is a large book with its share of longueurs, I did enjoy reading it.*

loquacious   *adj.* talkative: *I was happy to have that loquacious young actor at our table—I'm a terrible conversationalist myself.* Synonyms: **garrulous**, **voluble**.

loquaciousness   *n. I'd forgotten about the incredible loquaciousness of two year olds.*

losel   *n.* a worthless person: *How could she ever have thought she could find happiness with such a losel?*

louche   *adj.* questionable; shady, or disreputable: *I'd never been to this louche club before, and I won't be going back.*

lucent   *adj.* **1** shining, bright, or incandescent: *The lucent sun made my eyes ache.* **2** clear or transparent: *She gazed through the lucent waters at the rocks on the lake bottom.*
   lucency, lucence   *n.* brightness or incandescence: *The sky lit up, and the sea, changing color, took on a subdued lucency.*

lucid   *adj.* **1** easily understood; clear: *He proved to be an excellent companion who happily shared his lucid insights into the action unfolding before us.* **2** having full mental faculties; sane: *After the incident, he was never fully lucid, although the medication seemed to help.* **3** full of light: *The lucid sky woke me hours before I had intended to arise.*
   lucidity   *n.* clarity of thought, speech, or writing, or the ability to see the truth instantly: *Such lucidity is unexpected in writers so young.*

lucre   *n.* money; monetary reward: *There seems little doubt that lucre is a stimulus to workplace productivity.*

lugubrious *adj.* mournful, dismal, or gloomy: *He has a taste for gothic novels and lugubrious music.*
    lugubriously *adv. Several women sat with Mom, lugubriously keening throughout the afternoon and evening.*

luminous *adj.* **1** giving off or reflecting light, bright, or glowing: *We strolled along the beach by the light of a luminous full moon.* **2** exceptional, clear, or brilliant in composition or presentation: *a luminous novelization*
    luminously *adv.* brightly and giving off a soft glow: *Ordinary objects in these windows look luminously beautiful here because they are placed and lit so perfectly.*

luteous *adj.* greenish yellow or brownish yellow: *Walter shook out the cloth, then stood admiring the dust particles suspended in the attic's luteous air.*

luxuriant/luxurious see at L CONFUSABLES

M

CONFUSABLES

macabre/bizarre If something is *macabre*, it is gruesome, horrifying, or about death (*a macabre accident scene*); something *bizarre* is merely strange (*Some people at the party were dressed in bizarre outfits.*).

majority/plurality A *majority* is more than half (*The majority of human beings are female.*); a *plurality* is a number of votes that exceeds the number any other candidate receives, or the most votes in a context of three or more candidates in which no one gets more than half the votes (*It's possible to win a majority of the electoral votes while only winning a plurality of the popular vote.*); a *plurality* is also the number of votes by which one candidate outpolls another (*She won by a plurality of three hundred votes.*).

malfeasance/misfeasance   *Malfeasance*   is wrongdoing, especially when illegal or constituting official misconduct (*Opposition leaders accused Pentagon officials of malfeasance.*); *misfeasance* is the act of doing something legal and proper in an illegal and improper manner (*Sexual intercourse between a married man and woman becomes misfeasance when it happens on the steps of city hall.*).

malign/impugn To *malign* someone is to speak misleadingly about them, whether on purpose or not (*Lawyers are always maligning witnesses they hope to discredit*); if you *impugn* someone, you attack them (*Clinton was impugned by the Judiciary Committee.*).

meteor/meteorite A *meteor* is a piece of debris moving through or vaporized in the atmosphere, visible as a streak of light in the sky (*a meteor shower*); a *meteorite* is a piece of space debris that has landed on earth (*a trove of meteorites displayed in a museum*).

militate/mitigate To *militate* means to fight or have force (*a new campaign to militate against drug abuse*); to *mitigate* means to soothe or make less hostile (*He mitigated her anger by sending flowers.*).

moral/ethical see **ethical/moral** at E Confus-
ABLES

moron/idiot Technically, a *moron* is someone with a mental age of between eight and twelve, who is the least deficient of the mentally impaired; an *idiot* is someone with a mental age of up to three, who is the most deficient; in common usage, both words are used to signify a fool.

mutual/common *Mutual* means of each for the other or others, and describes something one person has (*There's a real mutual affection and respect on this team that you don't see in men's sports.*); *common* means shared, or belonging to all (*a common bathroom*); both words can be used to mean joint (*our mutual/common self-interest*).

mutual/reciprocal see **reciprocal/mutual** at R CONFUSABLES

---

macabre see at M CONFUSABLES

machination *n., usually pl.* **machinations** a cunning scheme or plot: *The article discusses various machinations used in the past to manipulate stock prices.*

madding *adj.* frenzied: *I could see Sean duck quickly into the house as a madding mass of wasps flew from the nest he'd knocked down.*

mage, magi *n.* see at **magus**

magus, mage *n., pl.* **magi** a magician or sorcerer: *Charisma is one of the more important characteristics of a magus.*

> A Magus is one of the three wise men—Balthazar, Caspar, and Melchior—the Magi who, according to the biblical tale, came to see the baby Jesus when He was born.

maidan *n.* an open space where concerts, markets, fairs, festivals, and other large public gatherings take place: *There's a flea market at the maidan on the east side every Saturday from May to October.*

maieutic *adj.* having to do with the Socratic method that causes someone to develop concepts by asking them a logical series of questions: *Conner's maieutic approach angered those students who expected to be told only that their answers were right or wrong.*

majolica, maiolica *n.* richly decorated earthenware with a tin oxide glaze, especially that made in Italy: *The pottery collection includes some especially lovely pieces of majolica.*

majority see at M CONFUSABLES

malaise *n.* **1** a sense of unease and discomfort, such as the feeling of coming down with an illness: *Although generally robust, even healthy as an ox, he nonetheless suffered this malaise every springtime.*

2 a sense of the decline or destruction of civilized life: *The decadent malaise and hedonism of the 60s and 70s gave way to a can-do, me-first attitude of materialism in the 80s.*

malevolent   *adj.* evil, or wishing harm or evil on others: *In post–World War II America, Soviet Communism was held to be the epitome of malevolent dictatorship.* ∗ *She turned bitter and malevolent.*
   malevolently   *adv. She laughed malevolently.*
   malevolence   *n.* hatred or ill will: *Clearly I had underestimated Karen's malevolence.*

malfeasance   see at M CONFUSABLES

malign   see at M CONFUSABLES; see also **benign/ malign** at B CONFUSABLES

malingerer   *n.* someone who pretends to be ill in order to avoid doing something, usually to avoid work: *The four malingerers, who were collecting disability insurance for faked injuries, have been charged with fraud.*
   malinger   *v. In the end, her malingering cost not just her job, but her career.*

mandarin   *n.* a bureaucrat, official, or member of a particular elite group: *Secretary Albright was counted among the foreign policy mandarins long before she was appointed Secretary of State.*

Within the Imperial Chinese government, prior to 1912, the mandarins were the members of the nine ranks of high public officials, each rank distinguished by a particular jeweled button worn on their caps. In China, these officials were actually known as *guan*: the word "mandarin" comes to us via Portuguese, and originally, Malay.

manifold   *adj.* having many different types, elements, reasons, or processes: *As editor, he must keep track of all the manifold elements of compiling, designing, and producing both the dictionary and the CD.*

manque   *n.* the low numbers in roulette, 1 through 18, or a bet made on these numbers. See also **passe**.

manqué   *adj.* would-be; wanting to be but not succeeding: *This woman was some sort of Barbie manqué, though why anyone would want to be Barbie for real was beyond me.* Manqué is always used after the noun it modifies.

manumit   *v.* to free or release someone from bondage or servitude: *At the beginning of the nineteenth century, substantial numbers of slaves were manumitted in the more northerly of the Southern states, such as Virginia and Maryland.*
   manumission   *n. In the deep South, there were few manumissions before the Civil War.* Compare **emancipate**, **emancipation**.

maquette   *n.* a small model, especially of a building or statue before it is made: *The service buildings were two stories tall, but viewed against the enormous structure they were servicing, they appeared to be mere maquettes.*

marl   *n.* earth consisting of clay and calcium carbonate: *He laid himself and his pack down on the marl and waited for the others to join him.*

marmoreal, marmorean   *adj.* like or having the characteristics of marble: *He showed no emotion, standing cool, placid, marmoreal, awaiting the judge's decision.*

massif   *n.* the spine of a mountain range: *With some sort of triangulatory calculation, he was able to assess the height of this massif.*

mattock   *n.* a type of digging tool that has a flat blade that forms a right angle with the handle

maunder   *v.* to move, act, or speak in an aimless or meandering fashion: *The minister maundered through the sermon, drifting between apparently disconnected topics without any concern for connecting them.*

melee   *n.* hand-to-hand fighting among a large group of people; turmoil: *The crowd rushed the intruders and a bloody melee began.*

memento mori   *phrase, pl.* **memento mori** "remember that you must die"; a reminder of death and mortality: *The attic was a trove of the memento mori that were once acceptable parlor decorations but these days are thought morbid or just plain weird.*

Words of Death

Memento mori means "remember you must die," and this list provides a reminder while also offering terms for places and pronouncements having to do with death and dying.

catafalque *n.* the platform or structure on which a body lies in state.

charnel *n.* a building or place where bodies or bones are put.
  charnel *adj.* pertaining to dead bodies.

cinerary *adj.* of or for the ashes of the dead.

columbarium *n.* a building or burial vault with recessed spaces to hold cremated ashes.

elegy *n.* a song or poem with a sad, contemplative tone, especially one suitable or written for the dead.

eulogy *n.* a speech or statement praising someone, especially someone who has died.

memento mori *phrase* "remember that you must die"; a reminder of death and mortality.

obsequy *n.* a funeral rite.

perimortem *adj.* happening or existing at the time of death.

sepulchre *n.* a tomb or burial place.
   sepulchral *adj.* suitable for a funeral; funereal.

mendacious *adj.* lying, dishonest, untruthful: *She was one of the most deceitful, mendacious people I ever met.*
   mendaciously *adv. He continued to mendaciously insist he'd been at the party, when we all knew it wasn't true.*
   mendaciousness *n.* a dishonest or untruthful attitude or quality: *His thoroughgoing mendaciousness makes his story difficult to swallow.*

mendacity *n.* a lie, or a dishonest or untruthful attitude or quality: *The love which prophets urged us to offer the stranger is the same love that Jean-Paul Sartre could reveal as the very mendacity of hell.*

mensuration *n.* the act of measuring, or the measurement of geometric figures: *These proportions can be discovered by mensuration.*

mercurial *adj.* **1** eloquent, spirited, and shrewd: *The governor—mercurial, intelligent, with a magnetic personality—presents herself better, and more favorably, than most of her party's other politicians.* **2** changing often and suddenly; volatile: *That mercurial temperament won't win you friends!*

merkin *n.* the vulva: *The paintings seemed to be abstract interpretations of a merkin.* **2** a pubic-hair wig for a woman: *Who could conceive of the need for a merkin?*

meretricious *adj.* **1** attractive and alluring in a false, showy, or tawdry way: *Kids putting up graffiti around town were simply playing out a fantasy of meretricious fame.* **2** seeming likely or believable but not true or real: *This meretricious testimony is designed to elicit sympathy from the jury, but it will be proven groundless.*

metastasize *v.* **1** to dangerously spread, or to change into something dangerous: *The candidate's homegrown mythos has metastasized within media circles and threatens to overwhelm the political reality.* **2** to spread disease to other parts of the body: *She feared the tumor would metastasize.*

meteor/meteorite see at M CONFUSABLES

métier *n.* a person's trade or profession; something a person is good at or well suited for: *Even I was surprised to find fund-raising to be my métier.* Compare **forte**.

miasma   *n., pl.* **miasmas, miasmata 1** an unhealthy atmosphere or influence: *We can only hope common sense—and strict gun-control laws—will prevail over the miasma of the gun culture in this country.* **2** a mist and odors rising from a swamp or decaying matter, once thought to be poisonous and responsible for diseases, especially malaria: *We took a daybreak canoe tour through the miasma of the Jersey meadowlands.*

micturate   *v.* to urinate: *Our dog wandered down the block, sniffing at every bush and micturating where it pleased.*

milieux   *n.* a milieu

militate   see at M CONFUSABLES

minatory, minatorial   *adj.* threatening: *When provoked, she became ever so slightly minatory.*

minim   *n.* **1** *esp. British* a half note **2** a unit of measure of fluids equal to ⅟₆₀ of a dram (0.0616 milliliters) in the United States and ⅟₂₀ of a scruple (0.0592 milliliters) in Great Britain **3** a small amount or insignificant thing: *There was a minim of interest in the show, but it was sold out.*

minimal   see **nominal/minimal** at N CONFUSABLES

misandry   *n.* hatred or distrust of men: *Her scathing attacks on male power were often misconstrued as outright misandry.*

misanthrope, misanthropist *n.* someone who doesn't like or trust people: *Never particularly outgoing, he became a reclusive misanthrope in middle age.*

   misanthropic, misanthropical *adj. Daily exposure to these nitwits leaves me feeling increasingly misanthropic.*

   misanthropy *n.* distrust or dislike of people: *Those who aren't given to misanthropy or self-indulgence can't get away with the pretense of meanness.*

misfeasance see **malfeasance/misfeasance** at M
CONFUSABLES

misogamy *n.* hatred of marriage: *Some of Noel Coward's plays suggest that misogamy is an acceptable attitude.*

misogyny *n.* hatred or distrust of women: *The kind of misogyny that had been commonplace in the locker room was no longer considered acceptable.*
   misogynist *n. She could cope with him if he were only an idiot, but when she realized he was also a misogynist, she knew she would have to quit.*

misology *n.* extreme dislike of logical argument, reason, or enlightenment: *Students today seem to have a deep-seated misology, preferring ignorance as long as it doesn't require any effort.*

misoneism   *n.* hatred or distrust of change or innovation: *His well-known misoneism led him to live an increasingly reclusive life.*

mithridate   *n.* an antidote to a poison, especially a sugar or syrup

mitigate   *v.* to lessen, or to make something less severe or less harsh: *If you'd only call when you know you will be late, it would mitigate his annoyance and anger.* See at M CONFUSABLES
  mitigation   *n. The defendant had agreed to provide information to the D.A. in the hope it would lead to some mitigation in his sentencing.*

mnemonic   *adj.* aiding memory, relating to memory or to a way of remembering something: *We came up with a few mnemonic tricks to help her remember all the elements on the periodic table. * I'm sure I did well on the mnemonic section of the test.*
  mnemonics   *pl., n.* a technique for remembering things or for improving memory: *I find mnemonics helpful for remembering formulas.*

monadnock   *n.* a mountain that stands alone; inselberg.

moral   see **ethical/moral** at E CONFUSABLES

morass   *n.* a confused, complex, and difficult situation: *I had no idea what a morass this project would turn out to be when I took the job six months ago.*

mordant *adj.* sarcastic or biting: *He told the story with uncommon liveliness and mordant wit.*

   mordantly *adv. They kept on, mordantly baiting each other throughout dinner.*

moron see at M CONFUSABLES

mortal *adj.* **1** extemely serious, dire, or difficult to forgive: *mortal terror* ∗ *This is a mortal offense.* ∗ *mortal sin* Antonym: **venial. 2** causing death, or able to die: *a mortal wound* ∗ *All of us are mortal.*

mortmain *n.* **1** ownership of real estate by institutions like churches that cannot transfer or sell it, or gifts left to such institutions in perpetuity **2** the influence of the past on the present, especially when considered an oppressive force: *This mortmain pervaded her life, forcing her always to do things as they are meant to be done, as they have always been done.*

mot juste *n., pl.* **mots justes** the right word: *"Perfect" is the mot juste to describe her performance.*

moue *n.* a pout or wry grimace: *That moue that flickered over his face told me he was feeling sorry for himself and could care less about what had happened to me.*

mufti *n.* ordinary clothes, especially when worn by someone who usually wears a uniform: *My companion was traveling in mufti, although other aspects* *of his bearing and appearance gave away his military background.*

mugwump   *n.* **1** an independent person or neutral party politics: *Americans are hopeless mugwumps, never willing to stick with a party through thick and thin.* **2** a Republican who left the party in 1884 over the presidential candidacy of James G. Blaine

muliebrity   *n.* **1** the state of being a woman **2** femininity: *For American women, not shaving our legs and under our arms affronts the narrow boundaries of muliebrity.*

mullion   *n.* a vertical piece of wood or other material dividing the panes in a window: *The window was destroyed—sash, mullion, and sill.*

munificence   *n.* something lavish, generous, or profuse: *Several old theaters have been rebuilt with all their marvelous ornateness restored, giving us a much-needed view of the munificence of our past.*
   munificent   *adj.* generous or showing generosity: *a munificent contribution*
   munificently   *adv. Carol munificently thanked all those who had helped her.*

muse   *v.* to think about or carefully consider something in a meditative way: *I'm not ready to comment on this newest proposal; I'd like to muse over it a bit.* Compare **brood**.

muse, Muse *n.* someone who inspires another person's creativity, or a goddess presiding over one of the arts: *Adrian is my Muse.* * *Tragedy is the domain of the Muse Melpomene.*

Goddesses of Art and Beauty

The original Muses of classical mythology were the three sisters Aoede (song), Melete (meditation), and Mneme (memory).

The goddess sisters most often referred to as the Muses, however, are those later described by Homer. They are the nine daughters of Zeus and Mnemosyne: Calliope, who presides over epic poetry; Euterpe, music and lyric poetry; Erato, love poetry; Polyhymnia, sacred poetry; Clio, history; Melpomene, tragedy; Thalia, comedy; Terpsichore, choral music and dance; and Urania, astronomy.

The companions of the Muses were the goddesses of charm and beauty known as *the Graces,* or Charities. These three sisters are the daughters of Zeus and Eurynome: Aglaia, Euphrosyne, and Thalia.

---

mutual see at M Confusables; see also **reciprocal/mutual** at R Confusables

myopic *adj.* **1** nearsighted: *You're developing a myopic squint.* **2** lacking a long-term view, shortsighted, narrowminded: *The museum leadership has become too myopic; they lack vision.*

myopia   *n.* *She has severe myopia.*

myriad   *n.* an indefinite number: *There were a myriad of new products on display at the electronics show.*

   myriad   *adj.* innumerable, or having a indefinite number of variations: *The myriad reflections in the mirrors resulted from their exact placement in relation to each other.*

myrmidon   *n.* a follower who carries out orders without question: *Nixon's myrmidons devised and carried out the cover-up strategy spearheaded by the president.*

mythogenic   *adj.* producing or able to produce myths: *To behave like an ill-tempered crank, and get invited to deliver more lectures, you need to develop a reputation as a grouch so entrenched that it becomes mythogenic.*

   mythogeny, mythogenesis   *n.* the production of myths: *He poked fun at the mythogeny of psychoanalysis throughout his life.*

mythopoeic, mythopoetic   *adj.* having to do with mythmaking: *It's unclear to me whether you can call a bad storyteller mythopoeic, unless you think of him as adding weight to the myth of the bad storyteller.*

mythos *n., pl.* **mythoi** beliefs; myth or mythology: *The candidate had come to believe the mythos of his own campaign slogans.* The plural form has fallen out of use almost entirely, and mythos is now heard in both singular and plural constructions.

N

CONFUSABLES

naught/aught see **aught/naught** at A CONFUSABLES

nauseated/nauseous *Nauseated* has historically been restricted to meaning sick to the stomach (*The smell nauseated me.*); *nauseous* means causing nausea or loathing (*a nauseous smell * a nauseous performance*); *nauseous* is also now commonly used to mean sick to the stomach (*I was feeling pretty nauseous.*)

nocturnal/diurnal see **diurnal/nocturnal** at D CONFUSABLES

nominal/minimal A *nominal* amount is small or insignificant (*The program charges a nominal fee.*); a *minimal* amount is the smallest possible (*There have been minimal casualties.*)

notable/notorious Something *notable* is remarkable and worthy of being known for its positive attributes (*a notable woman of the twentieth century*); something *notorious* is widely known for being bad (*a notorious criminal*).

---

naif, naïf *n.* someone inexperienced and naive: *My new assistant is a naif just out of school.*

nascent *adj.* just coming into being, starting, or beginning: *It was more of a nascent idea than a full-fledged plan at this point, but it was all they had.*
  nascence, nascency *n.* the quality of newness: *Spring, which provides such a visible metaphor for the processes of rebirth, growth, and resurrection, has become associated with other kinds of nascence.*

naught see **aught/naught** at A CONFUSABLES

nauseated/nauseous see at N CONFUSABLES

navvy *n. esp. British* a laborer: *Jack was one of the navvies who helped dig the tunnels for the London Underground.*

nefarious *adj.* wicked or evil: *You're wise to distance yourself from the nefarious dealings of that investment group—I understand the treasury department is investigating them.*

ne plus ultra *phrase* the best possible; the most perfect: *In the 1970s, the European tour ceased to be the ne plus ultra of college graduation gifts; "junior year abroad" and summer backpacking trips made affordable by cheap student airfares changed European travel into a virtual rite-of-passage for middle-class college kids.*

neurasthenic *adj.* seeming like or suffering from nervous exhaustion: *The stress of the children's death showed in her neurasthenic tone and the hyper-clarity of her memories.*

neurobiology *n.* the part of science that deals with the nervous system.
   neurobiological *adj. The complicated interactions of neurobiological and social factors make you who and what you are.*

nexus *n.* a link or central connecting point: *It's not the lab but the adjoining meeting room that is the real nexus of our research efforts.*

niggle *v.* **1** to fuss and spend a lot of time on less important details: *Look, I want to figure out the basic schedule today, not niggle about how many minutes are in a coffee break.* **2** to criticize in a petty way: *You can't please this committee; they'll always find things to niggle over.*
   niggling *adj.* trivial or unimportant: *Stop it with these niggling questions and what-ifs—it makes no difference!*

nihilism *n.* rejection of moral constraints and religious beliefs, and skepticism that there could be any meaning or purpose in existence: *What frightened people about the punk culture of the late 70s was its apparent nihilism.*
  nihilistic, nihilist *adj. Steve had become depressingly nihilistic, and I didn't want to see him anymore.* * *a nihilist worldview*
  nihilist *n. the attitudes of a nihilist*

nimbus *n.* **1** a circle of light surrounding someone's head, especially the head of a saint or royal person in a drawing: *She gazed at Mick up on stage, the backlit nimbus making him look deified.* **2** a thundercloud: *Gathering nimbuses threatened to wash away the picnic.*

noblesse oblige *phrase* the obligation of people with a high social position to behave with honor and generosity: *In some quarters, noblesse oblige has given way to petty stinginess.* * *Government does not always respond with noblesse oblige to the needs of citizens.*

nocturnal *adj.* being active and awake during the night, or happening during the night: *We went for a nocturnal walk down to the lake.* * *Few owls are diurnal, most are nocturnal.* See **diurnal/nocturnal** at D CONFUSABLES. Antonym: **diurnal**.

nolo contendere *phrase* "I do not contend"; a defendant's plea in a criminal case, often leading to conviction, whereby no defense is made or guilt admitted, allowing for a denial of guilt in related criminal proceedings: *Well, it seems my old broker has pleaded nolo contendere on two counts.*

nominal see at N CONFUSABLES

non compos mentis *adj.* mentally incompetent, and therefore not legally responsible or able to manage one's own affairs: *He had a knack for making the opposition look non compos mentis.*

nonplus *v.* to cause someone to be surprised, confused, or perplexed: *His special talent when he was nineteen was an ability to nonplus his professors at the drop of a hat.*
   nonplus *n.* a state of disorientation or confusion: *His nonplus over the sudden schedule change rendered him useless for the rest of the morning.*
   nonplused, nonplussed *adj.* surprised, confused, and disoriented: *She should have expected his proposal, but she was completely nonplused by it.*

nostrum *n.* a medicine of questionable usefulness, or an uncertain remedy for a problem: *The side effects of some of the nostrums of modern medicine leave you to wonder if the cure may be as bad as the disease.* * *When feeling sluggish and a bit down, my nostrum is a bowl of spinach, while Paul's is a long run.*

notable see at N CONFUSABLES

notorious see **notable/notorious** at N Confusables

nugatory *adj.* without meaning or value; worthless: *The experience of this incredibly expensive, lavish meal was nugatory.*

numen *n., pl.* **numina** a spirit, especially one considered to inhabit particular parts of nature or objects: *They left offerings for the numina of the waterfall.*

numinous *adj.* mystical, supernatural, or divine: *He felt as if they had undergone a numinous ritual, as if they had passed through an invisible door and been transformed.* * *The moon shone through the window, lighting the room with a numinous glow.*

O

CONFUSABLES

obligate/oblige Both words can be used to mean to force to do or restrain from doing (*We were obliged to leave when the lease expired.* * *She was obligated to prosecute him.*); *obliged* also means indebted or compelled by moral, ethical, or social forces (*I'm much obliged for your help.* * *He felt obliged to attend the meeting.*)

obscene/profane/vulgar All three terms describe things that are offensive; *obscene* material is offensive because of being lewd, indecent, and sexually arousing (*Police officers confiscated the obscene photographs.*); a *profane* act or person is offensive because of being disrespectful or irreverent toward God or religion (*The film's depiction of Christ was considered profane.*); if something is *vulgar,* it is offensive because it is crude, showy, or lacking in taste or manners (*a vulgar display of wealth*).

officious/official Someone *officious* is interfering or overly anxious to offer assistance (*Officious bureaucrats prevent us from getting the job done.*); if a diplomat does something *officious*, it is done without authorization (*My personal, officious response is that this will be bad for both parties.*); *official* means authorized and sanctioned (*an official NFL jacket*) or having to do with an office or position (*the official duties of the vice president*).

op. cit./ibid. see **ibid./op. cit.** at I CONFUSABLES

oppugn/impugn Both words mean to call into question or argue against; *oppugn* means simply to oppose (*She said she would oppugn me if I were to run for dog catcher.*); *impugn* means to argue against what is false (*I will impugn these slanderous accusations with all my strength.*).

optometrist/ophthalmologist/optician An *optometrist* is one who tests eyesight and prescribes corrective lenses; an *ophthalmologist* is a medical doctor who specializes in diseases and disorders of the eye; an *optician* is one who makes or sells corrective lenses.

outstanding/exceptional/egregious see **egregious/ outstanding/exceptional** at E CONFUSABLES

overlay/overlie   Both words mean to cover; *overlay* means to attach or place over (*Linoleum overlays the bare wood flooring.*); *overlie* means to spread upon or exist over (*Snow overlies the cold winter landscape.*).

overlook/oversee   To *overlook* means to observe from a higher place (*The house overlooks the sea.*), or to not observe, whether intentionally or not (*I'll overlook those remarks.*); to *oversee* means to supervise (*Managers oversee the production line.*).

---

obdurate   *adj.* stubborn in refusing to admit error, or resistant to influence by others: *She has a raven's heart, small and obdurate, uninterested in the concerns of the modern world.*

obeisance   *n.* **1** respect or honor shown to a superior: *I thought he was a lesser figure in the field, but I was more than willing to pay obeisance to even a minor god in the jazz pantheon.* **2** a movement expressing deference or homage, such as a bow or curtsy: *Leaving center court at the completion of the Wimbledon match, the competitors stop to make a quick obeisance in front of the royal box.*

obfuscate   *v.* to confuse, or to obscure: *These other issues obfuscate the concerns that need to be dealt with right now.*

obfuscation *n. Obfuscation will not keep the truth from coming out.*

oblate *adj.* having a shape that is flattened at the ends but otherwise rounded: *From his pocket he drew a magnificently decorated oblate spheroid whose purpose we could not even begin to guess.*

obligate/oblige see at O Confusables

obscene see at O Confusables

obsequious *adj.* fawning, servile, and compliant: *The staff struck me as uniformly obsequious, and I began to wonder if it was an intentional hiring policy.*
    obsequiously *adj. He bowed and smiled obsequiously and led us into the sitting room.*
    obsequiousness *n. I find her manner off-putting—her obsequiousness makes me nervous.*

obsequy *n.* a funeral rite: *Mike spoke at the obsequy for Pat, which took place at Saint Henry's, as had my mom's and dad's.*

obstreperous *adj.* noisy, boisterous, and unruly: *A group of obstreperous wedding guests was staying the night at a nearby motel, and they continued to party into the wee hours.*
    obstreperously *adv. The team obstreperously celebrated their victory in today's playoff.*
    obstreperousness *n. Angie easily dealt with the obstreperousness of a class of six year olds.*

obtrude *v.* to push out or thrust forward; intrude: *Several time-consuming, unrelated issues that had been obtruded into the discussion were finally set aside.*

obtuse *adj.* stupid, dull-minded, or slow to understand: *Don't be so obtuse, Donna, it's really a very simple concept. * The officer's eyes could chill even the most obtuse of felons.*
    obtuseness, obtusity *n.* stupidity: *For the artist there is little more frustrating than the obtuseness of patrons and art dealers.*

obverse *adj.* **1** facing or in the direction of the observer: *Please look closely at the obverse side of this vase.* **2** being opposite or complementary: *Consider the obverse side in this case—what would you do?*
    obverse *n.* **1** the "heads" side of a coin or medal, which has the principal design: *Check the obverse and reverse for any flaws that might reduce the coin's value.* **2** the more noticeable or likely of two alternatives: *A deficit is merely the necessary obverse of a surplus.* **3** in logic, an opposite proposition that changes a positive statement to a negative one: *The obverse of "every word is definable" is "no word is undefinable."*

obviate *v.* to anticipate and stop or prevent something, or to make something unnecessary: *Adequate preparation in high school would obviate the current remedial courses on entering college.*

Occam's razor *n.* the principle that the fewest number of assumptions should be made in trying to explain or understand something, or that the most likely explanation is the simplest: *When the situation begins to get this complicated, I find Occam's razor comes in handy.* See **parsimony**.

The principle of Occam's razor is named for the fourteenth-century philosopher William of Occam.

occiput *n., pl.* **occipita, occiputs** the back of the head or skull

occlude *v.* to close, cover, or block something: *Sightlines in some seats are obstructed by pillars that occlude parts of center stage.*

occultation *n.* a disappearance from view, especially the transit of one celestial body behind another so that for a time it is completely hidden from view on earth: *the occultation of Saturn * a lunar occultation*

octavo *n.* a sheet of paper folded three times to make eight leaves or sixteen pages, or a book with small pages: *A series of commemorative octavos will be published to mark the anniversary.* See also **folio, quarto, quire**.

odalisque, odalisk *n.* a concubine or female slave, or a representation of one: *Her arms and legs dangle, too gawky to be an odalisque, but delicious in their curves.*

oeuvre *n.* all the works produced by an artist, writer, or musical composer: *The most important part of any artist's oeuvre is the work he has yet to complete.*

Artistic Endeavors

The world of art and artists is embellished by a number of terms that themselves could be displayed on pedestals. Many of these terms are employed outside the art world to give an artistic feel to more commonplace activities.

chef-d'oeuvre *n.* an artistic or literary masterpiece.

chiaroscuro *n.* the light and shade in a picture or drawing.

grisaille *n.* a three-dimensional effect obtained in painting by using monochromatic gray patterns.

kouros *n.* a statue of a naked boy or young man standing with his hands by his sides and his left leg coming forward, which was typically made in ancient Greece.

oeuvre *n.* all the works produced by an artist, writer, or musical composer.

opuscule *n.* a minor, unimportant work.

pentimento *n.* a visible hint or trace of an earlier painting that can be seen through the surface of a finished painting as it ages.

putto *n.* a figure of an infant, male angel, or cherub in painting, sculpture, or decoration.

telamon *n.* a supporting column sculpted in the form of a male figure.

trompe l'oeil *n.* a painting style that creates the illusion of three-dimensional reality.

officious/official see at O CONFUSABLES

omen *n.* a prophecy of an outcome: *The sudden storm seemed to be a bad omen.* Synonym: **portent**.

ominous *adj.* indicating evil; threatening; relating to an omen: *The terse message left on my answering machine seemed ominous, and I was sure something terrible must have happened.* Compare **inauspicious; portentous**.
  ominously *adv. The house was ominously quiet.*

omphalos *n.* a central point: *During the long prime of the Spanish Main, Cuba was the geopolitical omphalos of the empire.*

oneiromancy   *n.* prophecy based on the interpretation of dreams: *The oneiromancy of early psychoanalytic theory seems laughable these days.*

onerous   *adj.* very difficult or troublesome; oppressive: *The onerous duties of a Washington wife have led more than one first lady to drink, drugs, and depression.*

onomatopoeia   *n.* the creation or use of a word that imitates the sound associated with the thing or action it refers to: *No one is sure if the word "bebop" is simple onomatopoeia, or if it had some deeper significance to those who first used it.*

ontology   *n.* a theory about existence and the nature of being, or a part of metaphysics that deals with existence: *My own ontology does not allow for the existence of a divine being, although I do accept that others may disagree.*
   ontological   *adj.* relating to the nature of reality, human existence, or the state of being alive: *He seems to be in a state of nearly pure ontological terror because his longtime companion is about to die.*

opacity   *n.* **1** a state of darkness, without clarity or transparency; impenetrability: *The opacity of the window shade made it impossible to tell day from night.* **2** a condition that is obscure or unintelligible: *Was the opacity of that explanation intentional?* See also **opaque.**

opaque *adj.* preventing light from penetrating; dark: *I bought opaque blinds to keep the late afternoon sun from reflecting off my computer screen.* **2** unclear; unintelligible: *His reasoning is opaque.* **3** dull and slow-witted: *How could she not know she's supposed to meet us here—she's not opaque.*

op. cit. see **ibid./op. cit.** at I CONFUSABLES

ophthalmologist see **optometrist/ophthalmologist/optician** at O CONFUSABLES

opine *v.* to express one's opinion: *The moderator opined about the panelists' lack of courtesy.*

opprobrium *n.* disgrace and humiliation: *In the 1950s, he risked opprobrium by opposing the long tradition of white supremacy that held sway in the South.*
  opprobrious *adj.* disgraceful; deserving of reproach for shameful actions or behavior: *Her conduct was clearly opprobrious.*

oppugn see at O CONFUSABLES

optician see **optometrist/ophthalmologist/optician** at O CONFUSABLES

optimistic see **hopeful/optimistic** at H CONFUSABLES

optometrist see at O CONFUSABLES

opuscule   *n.* a minor, unimportant work: *His dissertation examined the opuscule of a little-known Welsh poet.*

oracle   *n.* a person, place, or thing through which people communicate with a god, often through signs, or the communication that is received
   oracular   *adj. Anne worried what the sea birds' sudden oracular silence could mean, but it seemed to me the storm clouds on the horizon made it quite clear.*
   • Compare **omen, portent**.

orotund   *adj.* **1** pompous and pretentious: *We had to listen to yet another speech by the orotund attorney.* **2** clear, rich, and resonant: *His orotund baritone filled the hall.*

orrery   *n.* a device that represents the solar system with balls that move in the relative positions and directions of the planets: *He kept a marvelous clockwork orrery on the table, the motions of which he found oddly soothing.*

orthography   *n.* the art of arranging letters and symbols in writing to correctly represent the spoken language; spelling: *I think the orthography changes if it's a noun, so you'd take a "makeup," or a "make-up test."*
   orthographic   *adj. There are a number of orthographic differences between American and British English.*

os *n.* **1** *pl.* **ora** a mouth or an opening: *The os of the cave looked invitingly cool.* **2** *pl.* **ossa** a bone: *The ossa of the hand form a complex system that makes manual dexterity possible.*

osculate *v.* to kiss: *He osculated her hand, her shoulder, her neck, her clavicle.*
    osculation *n.* the act of kissing, or a kiss: *Her osculation was perfunctory.*

ossify *v.* to become hard like bone; or to become set and inflexible in habits or opinions; rigidify: *In later years she lost her sense of humor and ossified into a domineering matriarch.*

ostentatious *adj.* showy or pretentious in order to impress or to attract attention: *The wedding dinner was an extravagant, ostentatious affair, but the food and the music were quite good. * We ran into my ostentatious cousin at the restaurant, and he insisted on joining us for dinner.*
    ostentatiously *adv. Audrey is ostentatiously showing off her new car again.*
    ostentatiousness *n. The event was an incredible show of ostentatiousness and poor taste.*

ostracism *n.* banishment or exclusion from society or from a particular group: *The blacklisted writers endured not only loss of income, but ostracism and political harassment as well.*

outré *adj.* exaggerated or unconventional: *The lighting gave the scene an outré effect.* Compare **recherché**.

outstanding see **egregious/outstanding/exceptional** at E CONFUSABLES

overlay/overlie see at O CONFUSABLES

overlook/oversee see at O CONFUSABLES

overweening *adj.* conceited, overconfident, or arrogant: *On Saturdays, the local streets are taken over by these overweening drivers who forget to leave their competitiveness back at the office.*

P

CONFUSABLES

palate/palette/pallet The *palate* is the roof of the mouth or the sense of taste (*Gronk's discriminating palate was offended by the swill they served him.*); a *palette* is a board on which paints and pigments are mixed by painters, or a range of colors (*They used a palette of blues and greens in the bedroom.*); a *pallet* is a portable storage platform (*pallets piled high with relief supplies*), or a small, hard bed (*I slept on a pallet on the floor.*).

pardon/excuse Both words are used to ask for or give forgiveness; to *pardon* means to forgive for a criminal act (*President Ford pardoned Richard Nixon.*); to *excuse* means to allow an absence or exemption (*excused from jury duty*).

parricide/patricide *Parricide* is the murder of

one's mother, father, of other close relative, or one who kills a parent or close relative; *patricide* is the murder of one's father, or one who kills one's father.

pathos/bathos see **bathos/pathos** at B CONFUS-ABLES

pendant/pendent A *pendant* is something that hangs from something else (*A beautiful pendant of filigreed gold hung from a leather cord around his neck.*); *pendent* means over-hanging (*Pendent rocks perched ominously above our path.*), dangling (*ripe, pendent apples*), or awaiting decision (*Our case is still pendent.*); each word can be used as an alter-nate spelling for the other.

perceptive/insightful see **insightful/perceptive** at I CONFUSABLES

peremptory/preemptive *Peremptory* can mean stopping action (*a peremptory motion in Con-gress*), undeniable (*a peremptory conclusion based on the evidence*), urgent (*a peremptory phone call*), or arrogant (*a haughty, peremp-tory attitude*); *preemptive* can mean acting in advance to obtain something (*a preemptive bid*), or self-initiated (*a preemptive air strike on an unsuspecting foe*).

persecute/prosecute To *persecute* means to harass or annoy, especially because of a belief

(*He felt as if the media were trying to persecute him.*); to *prosecute* means to bring legal action against (*Violators will be prosecuted.*), or to carry on (*She promised to prosecute the investigation no matter where it leads.*).

perspective/prospective   A *perspective* is a particular view (*You can't see much from this perspective.*), or an opinion (*From my perspective, this dispute seems silly.*); *prospective* means likely to happen or begin (*prospective parents * a prospective employer*).

peruse/browse see **browse/peruse** at B CONFU-SABLES

petit/petite   *Petit* means of secondary importance or gravity (*petit larceny*) and is used mostly in legal contexts; *petite* means small and slender (*Michelle is a very petite woman— she's five feet tall and weighs less than ninety pounds.*).

phase/faze see **faze/phase** at F CONFUSABLES

piteous/pitiable/pitiful   All three words mean deserving or arousing pity (*the piteous/pitiable/ pitiful plight of the homeless*); *pitiable* and *pitiful* also mean arousing pity mixed with contempt (*a pitiable/pitiful attempt at conversation*).

plethora/abundance see **abundance/plethora** at A Confusables

plurality/majority see **majority/plurality** at M Confusables

podium/lectern see **lectern/podium** at L Confusables

possible/feasible see **feasible/possible** at F Confusables

possible/hypothetical see **hypothetical/possible** at H Confusables

possible/viable see **viable/possible** at V Confusables

practical/practicable *Practical* means prudent, efficient, or economical, and usually applies to people, acts, or things that exist or have happened (*A practical artist knows how to deal with the business world.*); *practicable* means feasible or apparently workable, and usually describes plans that have not yet been tried (*a practicable proposal*).

precipitate/precipitous As an adjective, *precipitate* means headlong, violently hurried, or hasty and reckless, and describes people or their activities (*a precipitate dash into a burning building*); *precipitous* is used only as an adjective, and means steep (*a precipitous drop in blood pressure*).

predominant/predominate *Predominant*, an adjective, means having the most importance or authority (*the predominant ballplayer of his generation*); *predominate*, a verb, means to prevail or dominate (*Trump predominated the New York real estate world.*).

prescribe/proscribe To *prescribe* means to write an order for the preparation and use of a therapeutic agent (*Doctor Tay prescribed bed rest.*); to *proscribe* means to forbid or prohibit (*The bill proscribed smoking in restaurants.*).

presumptive/presumptuous If something is *presumptive*, it is considered reasonable to accept or believe it (*He disputed her presumptive innocence.*); if something is *presumptuous*, it is arrogant (*It was presumptuous of you to think you could spend the night.*).

principal/principle A *principal* is the head of a school (*North is the principal of the Hommocks school.*), a main performer (*a principal with the NYC Ballet*), money lent or borrowed (*You barely start to pay off the principal on a mortgage in the first several years.*), or the main support in a building's frame; a *principle* is a moral rule or overarching law (*the accepted principle of doing unto others what you want done to you*).

profane/obscene/vulgar see **obscene/profane/ vulgar** at O CONFUSABLES

prognosis/diagnosis see **diagnosis/prognosis** at D CONFUSABLES

prone/supine If you are *prone* you are lying facedown; if you are *supine*, you are lying on your back.

---

pace *prep.* contrary to; despite the opinion expressed by: *I was independent, on my own, and, pace Bob Dylan, did not have to serve someone as far as I was concerned.*

paean *n.* a song or other expression of praise or triumph: *This paean to Gray's perseverance shows him to be worthy of further study.*

paladin *n.* a military leader: *The old paladins who had graced French bank notes have been replaced by buildings and artists.*

palate see at P CONFUSABLES

paleography *n.* ancient writings, the study and interpretation of ancient writings, or ancient writing itself: *an expert in Sumerian paleography ∗ We've found letters and accounts dating from the 1790s in the farm's old cellars, but whether it's the paleography or the handwriting, I cannot read them at all.*

palette/pallet see **palate/palette/pallet** at P CONFUS-
ABLES

palimpsest *n.* **1** a reused writing surface, such as
parchment, that contains an erased text which can
still be discerned beneath the writing of newer text:
*Experts studying the palimpsest believe the underly-
ing text may have been written in the fifth century.* *
*To touch an actual Archimedes palimpsest was like
being able to actually touch history.* **2** something
that has additional, different layers beneath its surface: *Her mind is a palimpsest, holding the texts she
has studied in layer after layer, with her memory
able to extract every item from whatever stratum
holds it.* Compare **pentimento**.

palindrome *n.* a word, phrase, sentence, or number that reads the same backward or forward:
*George loves palindromes, even timeworn ones like
"A man, a plan, a canal, Panama!"*
  palindromic *adj. palindromic names like Anna
  and Otto*

palpable *adj.* able to be touched or felt; having or
seeming to have corporeal reality: *He had a vision,
a religious visitation so real it was almost palpable.* *
*At the party, one question hung in the air, palpable
but unspoken—are they marrying because she is
pregnant?*
  palpably *adj. The air was palpably wet and
  dense.*
  Antonym: **impalpable**.

pandemic   *n.* a disease that has become prevalent throughout large areas: *Asia is carefully watched for new flu strains because the last two pandemics originated in China.*
   pandemic   *adj.* widespread; generally prevalent: *pandemic tuberculosis * pandemic recession*
   Compare **endemic**; **epidemic**.

paradigm   *n.* an example or pattern that can be followed: *Spock's famous book served as a parenting paradigm that, for many years, was followed unquestioningly.*
   paradigmatic   *adj. We were entertained by his broad Southern drawl, but it was not the sort of paradigmatic pronunciation we wanted our students to emulate.*

pardon   see at P Confusables

parlous   *adj.* dangerous, unstable, or perilous: *The parlous state of the local economy has the financial community nervous.*

paroxysm   *n.* a sudden outburst or attack: *The audience convulsed in paroxysms of laughter.*

parricide   *n.* the killing of a parent or other close relative, or a person who commits such a murder: *Assassination of the president is tantamount to committing national parricide. * The brothers are convicted parricides who murdered both of their parents.* See at P Confusables.

parse *v.* **1** to analyze a sentence or describe a word in terms of grammar, part of speech, or syntax: *He carefully parsed each sentence in the essay but offered no opinion on the subject matter.* **2** to break into parts in order to closely examine and analyze: *The report is being parsed as if it were a novel, supplied with all the characteristics of a classic work of fiction.*

parsimony *n.* thrift or cheapness, or economy in achieving an objective, especially by following the principle of Occam's razor: *Renowned for his personal parsimony, he nonetheless endowed foundations that have spent his money extravagantly.* ∗ *Following the principle of parsimony, she sought to explain the unexplained by starting with the simplest possibility.*
    parsimonious *adj. The most parsimonious explanation is often the most likely to be the right one.*

Parthian *adj.* delivered while retreating or made while departing: *She put on a Parthian burst of speed.* ∗ *His Parthian shot was a nasty comment about the idiots running his department.*

parvenu *n.* a person of recently gained success, wealth, or power who is not yet comfortable in or not accepted by others in this social or economic class: *He's a young man who rose quickly and has the parvenu's brashness and insecurity, but he'll adjust.* Compare **arriviste**.

passe   *n.* the high numbers in roulette, 19 through 36, or a bet made on these numbers
　See also **manque**.

passé   *adj.* **1** not current or in fashion; out-of-date: *Their music, in fact, their whole style, is passé.* **2** a movement in ballet where one leg crosses behind or in front of the other

patent   *adj.* obvious; clear: *The letter was a patent forgery.*
　patently   *adv. Ann's version of events seemed patently true.*

pathos   *n.* pity, compassion, or the evocation of sympathy: *To hear of someone's suffering arouses her pathos, but to see it galvanizes her to take action.* See **bathos/pathos** at B Confusables.

patinate   *v.* a film or discoloring caused by the oxidation of a metal: *The copper roofing will turn green as it patinates.*

patois   *n., pl.* **patois** a regional variation of a language that differs from the language's standard form; a dialect: *It was several weeks before I began to develop a reasonable understanding of the local patois.* * *the patois of southern Louisiana*
Compare **creole**; **pidgin**.

patriarch   *n.* the male head or founder of a family, group, community, or organization, or the leading member of a group or community: *Gaudi was indisputably one of Barcelona's grand patriarchs.*

patrician *adj.* aristocratic and refined, or belonging to an aristocrat or noble: *Behind that patrician wall is a wild gothic garden.*
   patrician *n.* a senatorial aristocrat, or a citizen, noble, or administrator in ancient Rome

patricide see **parricide/patricide** at P CONFUSABLES

paucity *n.* small or inadequate in number or quantity; scarce: *The paucity of resources where the reservation was located is obvious.*

pedagogy *n.* the science of teaching, or the work of a teacher: *I can tell by the teacher's pedagogy that she studied at Bank Street.*
   pedagogical, pedagogic *adj. The school trains teachers with a particular pedagogical perspective.*
   pedagogically *adj. The program's methodology seems pedagogically sound.*

pedant *n.* **1** someone who shows off his or her learning, especially in public: *He is a pedant, but that is actually a benefit for a tour guide.* **2** someone who rigidly interprets and follows formal rules or gives excessive credence to book learning over experience and common sense: *At the risk of being labeled a pedant, I have to point out that we decided a policy for this less than a year ago.*

pedantic   *adj. a pedantic lecturer ∗ Don't try to be pedantic—the company appreciates creative ideas.* Synonym: **didactic**.

pedantry, pedanticism, pedantism   *n. She makes her points clearly and succinctly, without resorting to pedantry.*

pediment   *n.* a gable or cornice: *I want to photograph the ornate pediments above the doorways in this row of soon-to-be demolished townhouses.*

pedimented   *adj. The view is of a pedimented office building built at the turn of the century.*

pelagic   *adj.* having to do with the ocean: *The Marine Fisheries service is not the only institution with scientific knowledge of pelagic issues. ∗ Michael, a birding enthusiast, went on a cruise in the hope of seeing pelagic raptors native to the northwestern coast of North America.* Compare **bathypelagic**.

Sea Words

Oceans make up most of the earth's surface, and for many land-dwellers, it's all just sea. But oceanographers have divvied up both the water and the land beneath the water according to depth.

The **pelagic region** is the open waters of the ocean, while the **benthic region** is the ocean floor. The following terms are used to describe the different parts of each.

The **pelagic region** encompasses these designations:

epipelagic from a depth of 0–200 meters.

mesopelagic from a depth of 200–1,000 meters.

bathypelagic from a depth of 1,000–4,000 meters.

absyssopelagic from a depth of 4,000–6,000 meters.

hadopelagic from a depth of 6,000 meters to the base of ocean trenches.

The **benthic region** encompasses these designations:

supralittoral including land above high tide that is ocean-influenced.

littoral including land between low and high tide.

sublittoral including land from low tide to the edge of the continental shelf, 0–200 meters.

bathyal including land from the edge of the continental shelf to about 4,000 meters.

> **abyssal** including land from about 4,000 meters
> to about 6,000 meters.
>
> **hadal** including the deepest part of the ocean,
> below 6,000 meters.
>
> **Thalassic** waters are those in inland seas.

pendant/pendent see at P CONFUSABLES

penitential   *adj.* repentant or self-mortifying: *She dressed in a bundle of smocks and vests and penitential hangings.*
   penitentially   *adv. The two teens were grounded, and this afternoon they labored penitentially, mowing the lawn and weeding the flower beds.*

pensive   *adj.* thoughtful, serious, and expressing a little sadness: *The piano pieces were gentle and pensive, a big change from the turbulent operas they'd listened to earlier.*

pentimento   *n., pl.* **pentimenti** a visible hint or trace of an earlier painting that can be seen through the surface of a finished painting as it ages, or the layers underlying someone's personality: *The pentimento indicates that this pastoral landscape may have started its life as an altogether different scene.* Compare **palimpsest**.

penultimate   *adj.* relating to that which is next to the last or to something immediately before a final element or part: *The factory was known to produce* *the penultimate chemical to the manufacture of VX nerve gas.* Compare **antepenultimate**.

perceptive see **insightful/perceptive** at I CONFUSABLES

percipience, percipiency   *n.* keen perception: *She seemed to always understand just what was needed, her percipience never failing to astonish him.*

percipient   *adj.* having or displaying the power of keen perception: *His irony was lost on most of the audience, but at least one percipient attendee chuckled appreciatively.* Antonym: **impercipient**.

peregrination   *n.* a journey, often one made by walking: *I followed the crosstown peregrinations of my new acquaintance, from party to dinner to disco to nightclub.*

peremptory see at P CONFUSABLES

perfidy   *n.* deceit; a deliberate breaking of promises or of one's word: *Her perfidy lost her some friends, but not the election.*
   perfidious   *adj.* treacherous; deliberately faithless or deceitful: *An alliance with such a perfidious partner was a disastrous mistake.*

performative   *adj.* **1** having to do with a word or phrase that, by saying it, performs the action it describes: *"Congratulations" is a performative verb.* **2** having to do with action rather than thought: *As* *a people, Brits have never been good at the more contemplative arts, but they excel at the more performative art forms, like theater and gardening.*

perimortem   *adj.* happening or existing at the time of death: *The bones showed evidence of perimortem breaks.*

peripatetic   *adj.* traveling about from place to place: *After eighteen years in one place, we went through a peripatetic period, moving five times in four years.*

peripeteia, peripetia   *n.* a sudden change of fortune or circumstance, especially in literature: *Bob's decision to leave was the peripeteia on which the plot turned.*

pernicious   *adj.* extremely harmful; deadly: *This so-called review of distribution systems is nothing more than a pernicious scheme to defraud unsuspecting clients.*

perorate   *v.* to make a long, grandiloquent speech: *One of the most impressive things about him is his ability to perorate on almost any subject.*
    peroration   *n.* a long and pompous speech: *I'd begun wondering if the concert would ever start, when the principal finally ended her peroration and introduced the orchestra.*

perse   *adj.* of a dark gray-blue or bluish black color: *Jeanne's jet-black hair set off the perse scarf she was wearing around her neck.*

persecute see at P Confusables

perspective see at P Confusables

perspicacity *n.* clear understanding, good judgment, and fine perception: *The perspicacity of an astute member of the copy department led to the last-minute revisions that saved the editors and management embarrassment and possibly a lawsuit.*
    perspicacious *adj.* having or showing discernment; perceptive: *a perspicacious lawyer*

perspicuity *n.* clearness and lucidity: *The committee have not yet voted on implementation, but they were impressed by the perspicuity of the proposal.*
    perspicuous *adj.* clearly expressed or easily understood: *The technical aspects of the research are complicated, yet the presentation was perspicuous and easy to follow.*

pertinacious *adj.* tenacious; stubbornly resolute; obstinate: *He is both dedicated and pertinacious, but that doesn't make him right.*

peruse see **browse/peruse** at B Confusables

petit/petite see at P Confusables

petroglyph, petrograph *n.* writing or a picture carved into rock: *She spends her summers hiking through the wilderness of southern Utah, searching for petroglyphs left by long-gone civilizations.*

petulant   *adj.* showing annoyance or irritation: *She answered in a petulant tone, as if she could barely be bothered to grace us with a reply.*

phalanx   *n., pl.* **phalanxes 1** a compact, closely arranged group of people, animals, or things: *At the end of every movie, whole phalanxes of names and titles come charging downward on the screen.* **2** a close military formation in ancient Greece of soldiers with their shields overlapping and spears extended: *an attacking phalanx*

phantasm   *n.* something imagined; an illusion or a ghost: *He questions the reality of God, suggesting He may be only a phantasm believed in by the very young and the very old.*

    phantasmagoric, phantasmagorical   *adj.* bizarre, fantastic, or imagined: *In the solid world of business, it is not easy for the phantasmagoric to gain the upper hand.*

    phantasmal, phantasmic, phantasmical   *adj.* illusory, imaginary, or unreal: *You hardly know what to say to him because he's always taking offense at some phantasmal slight.*

phase   see **faze/phase** at F Confusables

philanthropy   *n.* the altruistic donation of money and other types of support to the needy, or for social, educational, or research purposes: *These ap-*

peals to community, conscience, and philanthropy seem contrary to the prevailing me-first ethos of the times.

philistine *n.* someone who is without intellectual or cultural interests, or who is indifferent or hostile to art and culture: *Alan is a committed philistine with zero interest in opera or ballet.*

    philistine *adj.* lacking intellectual or artistic interests; conventional: *a philistine attitude ∗ philistine taste*

    philistinism *n.* indifference to anything cultural or intellectual: *He was mistaken in thinking he could escape provincial philistinism by moving to the city.*

philoprogenitive *adj.* **1** producing large numbers of offspring: *Carol's philoprogenitive family produced eleven children in her generation, and there are thirteen and counting in the next one.* **2** having to do with the love of children in general, or of your own children: *It was her philoprogenitive nature that led Jean to work in early childhood education.*

physiognomy *n.* the physical features of someone or something, especially a person's facial features when considered as an outward manifestation of the person's character and personality: *For people on the roller coaster of fame, there is a sort of physiognomy of success, a countenance that accompanies good fortune.*

picaresque   *adj.* relating to or being an adventurer; roguish: *With her picaresque hero as guide, she is led into the strange subculture of orchid collectors and propagators.*

pidgin   *n.* a language combining elements of two or more languages that developed as a form of communication between peoples who speak different native languages and that has a less formal and developed structure and grammar than a creole: *Everyone in the city speaks the pidgin that developed as a trading language.* ∗ *Neither of us spoke the other's language, but over a bottle of wine we discussed the state of the world with pidgin and arm waving.* Compare **creole; patois.**

pillory   *v.* to publicaly ridicule a person or her or his ideas: *Referring to unfavorable representations in the press, he declared, "I have been pilloried without cause."*

pilose, pilous   *adj.* covered with soft, fine hairs: *He loved the way a shiver would make all the hairs on the downy, pilous nape of her neck stand on end.*

pinchbeck   *n.* **1** a zinc-copper alloy used for imitation gold **2** something made to resemble a more valuable item; a counterfeit: *I thought I was buying a piece of art, not some masquerading pinchbeck.*
　　pinchbeck   *adj.* **1** made of a zinc-copper alloy **2** fake; spurious: *These were worthless, pinchbeck coins.*

piquant *adj.* **1** pleasantly stimulating or curious; interestingly provocative: *She can be depended on to deliver a lecture that is intelligent, piquant, well thought-out.* **2** having a pleasingly sharp, tangy flavor; tart: *For dessert Paul served a delightfully piquant poached pear with lemon.*

piteous see at P Confusables

pith *n.* **1** the essential or significant part of something, or significance: *The pith of the agreement is paragraph three.* **2** the soft core of some types of plant stems, or the fibrous, white matter under the peel of a citrus fruit

pithy *adj.* brief and meaningful: *Mike can always be counted on for a few pithy comments about politics and current events.*

pitiable see **piteous/pitiable/pitiful** at P Confusables

pitiful see **piteous/pitiable/pitiful** at P Confusables

plaintive *adj.* expressing sorrow or sadness; melancholy: *She had such a plaintive look as she waved to the departing bus taking her friends away to summer camp.*

plaintively *adv. I heard someone calling plaintively and realized a child had accidentally locked herself in the bathroom.*

planetesimal *n.* one of the small orbiting bodies in space that, in some theories, come together to form the planets of the solar system: *There are some who believe Pluto should be classed as a planetesimal, not a planet, on the basis of its relatively small size.*

plangent *adj.* having a deep, resonant sound: *He's known for the plangent tone of his saxophone soliloquies.*

platitudinous *adj.* commonplace or trite, like a platitude: *I found the piece platitudinous, lacking the moral scope and humanity needed from art.*

plethora *n.* a large amount or number; an overabundance: *Ask the waiter to guide you through the plethora of dishes listed on the menu.* See **abundance/plethora** at A CONFUSABLES.

plurality see **majority/plurality** at M CONFUSABLES

podium see **lectern/podium** at L CONFUSABLES

polemic *n.* an argument attacking a position or opinion, especially about political and social issues: *The polemic from both sides made reasonable debate impossible.*

polemic, polemical *adj. Polemical grandstanding has disrupted every attempt to find a compromise.*

polemics *pl. n.* the art or practice of arguing controversial issues: *Polemics is an asset for any would-be legislator.*

polemicist, polemist *n.* someone skilled in arguing controversial issues: *I wasn't aware of her talents as a polemicist before this morning's panel discussion.*

polemicize *v.* to encourage or create dispute and controversy: *We don't want to polemicize this, just make a simple schedule change.*

pollard *n.* a tree with the top branches removed, encouraging denser growth: *I knew every gate, hedge, path, and pollard on the farm.*

   pollarded *adj. I walked through the tidy district of stucco bungalows and pollarded trees.*

polymorphous, polymorphic *adj.* having or going through a variety of forms or stages; changing: *His polymorphous compositions dart back and forth, at times bright and cheering and at others, lugubrious and somber.*

   polymorphously, polymorphically *adv.* changeably; varyingly

polymorphous perverse *adj.* having nonspecific or nondirected sexual tendencies: *In my literature seminar, we are examining polymorphous perverse characterizations in some of Kafka's stories.*

Ponzi, Ponzi scheme   *n.* a financial swindle in which the investment capital of new investors is used to pay off previous investors until the scheme collapses because there are no new investors; also called a **pyramid scheme:** *The collapse of dozens of Ponzi schemes in Albania in the late nineties led to rioting and a nationwide financial crisis.*

> The Ponzi is eponymously named for Charles Ponzi, who made $15,000,000 in 1920 from his Boston-based scheme before it collapsed.

porcine   *adj.* like or of pigs and hogs; piggish: *I couldn't believe the people at the next table—you don't expect porcine table manners in a good restaurant.*

portent   *n.* **1** a sign or symbol of things to come: *June had always believed that a bird in the house was a portent of impending death.* **2** significance: *Lenny stood before his audience, letting them watch him, letting the moment draw meaning and portent without saying a word.* Synonym: **omen.**
   portentous   *adj.* **1** indicating evil or bad news: *Their alliance was portentous for their opponents.* Compare **inauspicious; ominous. 2** marvelous, wonderful, awe-inspiring: *After trying to conceive a child for more than five years, they viewed their baby's birth as a portentous event.*

posit   *v.* to assume something as fact: *No one seems to posit a future in which technology is the* *anodyne for poverty and ignorance.* ∗ *The plan posits a return of 3 percent in year one, increasing to 12 percent by year five.*

possible see **feasible/possible** at F CONFUSABLES; see also **hypothetical/possible** at H CONFUSABLES; see also **viable/possible** at V CONFUSABLES

postprandial *adj.* occurring after a meal: *Steve enjoyed a postprandial brandy on the porch.* Compare **prandial**.

postulant *n.* a candidate for membership in a religious order: *The old nun had been rising before dawn since her days as a postulant.*

powers *n.* the fourth of nine orders of angels. See THE CELESTIAL HIERARCHY at **angel.**

practical/practicable see at P CONFUSABLES

pragmatism *n.* a practical approach: *The early idealism of the program gave way to the pragmatism of younger members, products of a more conservative educational environment.*
    pragmatic *adj.* practical; realistic: *The executive committee adopted a more pragmatic approach to conference design.*

prandial *adj.* having to do with a meal: *Every holiday brings another prandial celebration of family togetherness.* Compare **postprandial.**

precedent   *n.* a decision that sets a way of deciding all similar questions: *The chairman stated that this decision should not be considered a precedent in future deliberations.* ∗ *This is a new field, but we can draw on the precedents of other entrepreneurial businesses in seeking investors.*

preciosity   *n.* meticulousness, or extreme refinement: *The art critic, whose preciosity is alternately lauded and reviled, holds a difficult position in the art world.*

precipitant   *adj.* sudden and hasty: *The fellow made such a precipitant exit that everyone began to laugh.*
　precipitantly   *adv. Andy was caught by surprise and jumped back so precipitantly, he stepped on his brother, who was right behind him.*

precipitate   *adj.* 1 dangerously or frighteningly fast: *A precipitate drop in blood pressure can signal a major coronary event.* 2 steep: *He hurtled down the precipitate slope at speeds that absolutely terrified me.* See at P Confusables
　precipitately   *adv.* 1 quickly: *The water level in this pond falls precipitately in the summer, draining away at a rate of almost a foot a week.* 2 steeply: *From here, the path drops precipitately to the floor of the valley.*

precipitate/precipitous see at P Confusables

predilection *n.* an inclination toward or a liking or preference for something: *a predilection for Italian films* ∗ *That kid has a predilection for trouble.*

predominant/predominate see at P Confusables

preemptive see **peremptory/preemptive** at P Confusables

prefigure *v.* to show by means of something similar a thing that is to come: *As it turned out, that three-month college stay in the British Isles prefigured two years of research in England almost a decade later.*

prehensile *adj.* relating to a body part that an animal can wrap around or grasp something with: *Using my prehensile big toe, I was able to top up the level of hot water in the tub without moving the rest of me.*

prelapsarian *adj.* relating to an innocent or carefree time: *The author regales us with joyful tales of his own prelapsarian youth in this semiautobiographical schooldays novel.*

In Biblical studies, prelapsarian refers to the period before Adam and Eve's fall from grace.

prepossessing *adj.* leaving a favorable impression, or attractive and engaging: *A prepossessing group* *of youngsters gathered at the large table near the front of the ice cream parlor.*

presage   *v.* to predict, foretell, or portend: *Their fights were vicious, rancorous affairs that seemed to presage a bad end to their relationship.*

prescience   *n.* foresight; knowledge of things that haven't yet happened: *He showed an eerie prescience about the uses of multiculturalism by cynical pols.*
   prescient   *adj. His staff seemed prescient, anticipating each move and acting together like a well-oiled machine.*

prescribe see at P CONFUSABLES

presentiment   *n.* a feeling that something is going to happen; a premonition: *I knew Kerrie wasn't expected, but I had a feeling she would come anyway, and Ann-Marie said she had the same presentiment.*

prestidigitation   *n.* deceptive movement; sleight-of-hand: *The U.N. inspectors were victims of a sort of national prestidigitation, with agencies around the country hiding crucial evidence of a military buildup.*

presumptive/presumptuous see at P CONFUSABLES

preternatural   *adj.* abnormal, extraordinary, or supernatural: *Ann has a preternatural understanding* *of the complexity of environmental regulation.* * *an athlete with preternatural skill and grace*

preternaturally *adv. I awoke, unsure of where I was; it was preternaturally quiet outside, which made me extremely nervous.* * *The media have been preternaturally inclined to praise everything digital, whether it makes sense or not.*

priapic, priapean *adj.* phallic, suggestive of a phallus, or overly concerned with masculinity: *a priapic monument* * *Relax—there just isn't any reason for this priapic insecurity.*

primeval, primaeval *adj.* relating to the first age; of the very earliest of times: *Fernbank forest in Atlanta is the only piece of virgin, primeval forest between Alabama and New York.* Compare **primordial.**

primordial *adj.* formed first, essential or original, or existing at the beginning: *Primordial germ cells were used in the research.* * *a primordial impulse.* Compare **primeval.**

principal see at P CONFUSABLES

principalities *n.* the third of nine orders of angels See THE CELESTIAL HIERARCHY at **angel.**

principle see **principal/principle** at P CONFUSABLES

prion *n.* a protein particle that can cause disease: *Degenerative brain diseases believed to be caused by* *prions include scrapie in sheep, mad cow disease, wasting disease in deer and elk, and Creutzfeldt-Jakob disease in humans.*

prion *adj. The experiment will use breeding stock in which prion disease has never been seen.*

privation *n.* the act of keeping something necessary from someone, or the state or condition of doing without something necessary: *People of a certain age can still recount the privations they suffered in the Great Depression of the 1930s.*

probity *n.* honesty and integrity: *Probity is as important as knowledge of the law in candidates for the judiciary.*

proclivity *n.* a natural tendency or propensity: *His proclivity for controversy has worked to his benefit this time.*

proconsul *n.* the administrator appointed to govern an occupied or dependent territory: *Following World War II, there were American proconsuls in both Germany and Japan.* ∗ *A proconsul will likely be needed in the area once the treaty is signed.*

In the ancient Roman Republic, proconsuls were governors or military commanders of the provinces, who held local executive power similar to that of the two consuls in Rome. The Roman consuls, elected annually, were the chief executives of the Republic, and former consuls were also called "proconsul."

procrastination *n.* delay, the act of putting something off until a later time: *These ongoing delays seem to be part of a policy of procrastination intended to dissuade people from continuing with their applications.*

profane see **obscene/profane/vulgar** at O CONFUS-ABLES

profligate *adj.* **1** wasteful, reckless, or extravagant: *He has sound ideas, but he's a profligate businessman so his backers pulled out and the company folded.* **2** indulgent, shameless, and indifferent: *She considered her new neighbors—the squatters who had moved into the empty building next door—profligate, irresponsible hedonists.*

progeny *n.* offspring or descendants, or someone or something that follows: *It was left to the courts to decide if the men were the progeny and rightful heirs.* * *writers who have no literary progeny*

prognosis see **diagnosis/prognosis** at D CONFUS-ABLES

prognosticate *v.* to make a prediction based on some sign or indication: *He prognosticates trends in the currency markets, and makes a lot of money at it.*

prognostication *n.* a prediction or prophecy: *He uses the Tarot to make his prognostications.* ∗ *I need more information before I can give you my prognostication.*

prognosticator *n.* someone who makes predictions; a fortuneteller. Compare **divination**.

Prophecy

As Yogi Berra once said, "It's hard to make predictions, especially about the future." But that certainly hasn't prevented prognostication from adding a plethora of difficult words to the modern lexicon.

If you are an **augur, diviner, prognosticator, soothsayer,** or **sibyl,** you can **augur, divine, foretell, presage,** or **prognosticate** by means of **augury, divination, geomancy, oneoromancy,** or **prescience** based on a **harbinger, portent, presentiment,** or **oracle.**

prognostication *n.* a prediction or prophecy.

augur *v.* to predict; point to.

divine *v.* to predict or foretell.

foretell *v.* to prophesy or predict.

presage *v.* to predict, foretell, or portend.

prognosticate *v.* to make a prediction based on some sign or indication.

augury   *n.* **1** the ability to make predictions **2** a sign or omen.

divination   *n.* the foretelling of the future; prophecy or fortune-telling.

geomancy   *n.* the art or ability of telling the future by means of lines and figures or by geographic features.

oneoromancy   *n.* prophecy based on the interpretation of dreams.

prescience   *n.* foresight; knowledge of things that haven't yet happened.

harbinger   *n.* something that foretells of something to come.

portent   *n.* a sign or symbol of something to come.

presentiment   *n.* a feeling something is going to happen; a premonition.

oracle   *n.* a person, place, or thing through which people communicate with a god, often through signs, or the communication that is received.

prolegomenon, prolegomena   *n., pl.,* **prolegomena**
a preliminary discussion, as an introductory essay;
opening remarks; preface: *The request to the Park
Service is a fifty-page prolegomena citing the problems the proposed excavation could solve and laying
out protocol and timetables.*

promiscuous   *adj.* **1** mingled together, indiscrimi-
nate, or haphazard: *In later years, the company suffered as a result of the promiscuous acquisitions of
an incompetent management team.* **2** having a large
number of casual sexual partners: *In her younger
days, she had been fairly promiscuous, even by the
standards of the time.*
　　promiscuity   *n.*   promiscuous   sexual   behavior:
The film focused on the promiscuity of the 70s.

promulgate   *v.* to publish, declare, announce, or
proclaim something; to make known publicly or officially: *We hope that rumors promulgated in organi-
zational   newsletters   and   circulating   among
committee members will be recognized for what they
are   and   not   affect   the   outcome   of   tomorrow's
meeting.*

pronate   *v.* to bend the hand so the palm faces
back or down, or to bend the foot down and in:
*The priest pronated his hand over their heads, offer-
ing the blessing of the Lord upon them.*

prone   *adj.* lying facedown, on one's stomach: *We
found him prone on the floor where he had passed*

out from the heat. Prone is sometimes used to mean lying down. See at P CONFUSABLES. Compare **recumbent**. Antonym: **supine**.

propitiate *v.* to appease someone, or to make someone favorably inclined toward you: *This man has been a big customer and we need his business, so he'll have to be propitiated.*

propitious *adj.* indicating or showing favorable circumstances: *The early arrival of the crew was propitious, and we looked forward to success in the day's racing.*

prosaic *adj.* **1** commonplace; ordinary and matter-of-fact: *Dealing with e-mail may be prosaic, but at the end of even a short vacation it can be daunting.* **2** relating to prose rather than poetry: *The school literary journal usually receives mostly prosaic submissions, but lately we're getting more poetry.*

proscribe see **prescribe/proscribe** at P CONFUS-ABLES

prosecute see **persecute/prosecute** at P CONFUS-ABLES

prospective see **perspective/prospective** at P CON-FUSABLES

protean *adj.* changeable; variable: *She was always protean, hidden, unknowable.*

prototypical   *adj.* of the type or model that others are based on: *Levittown was the prototypical postwar suburban housing development.* Synonym: **archetype.**

proximate   *adj.* **1** nearby, or at the closest point: *The moon looked huge and proximate.* **2** almost correct; roughly accurate: *If you don't know the exact amount, you can give a proximate figure.*
   proximity   *n.* nearness: *The residents object to the proximity of the new store to their neighborhood.*

prurience   *n.* an interest in or inclination toward lust and lasciviousness: *Perhaps it is the prurience of the public at large that has made daytime soap opera an ongoing success.*
   prurient   *adj.* appealing to sexual feelings, especially in an unwholesome way: *Does the mayor really think hiding sex shops on the fringes of town will somehow do away with prurient activities?*

psychosomatic   *adj.* relating to physical effects having a psychological or emotional cause: *It was beginning to look like his symptoms were psychosomatic, but now they've found he has a rare bacterial infection and started him on an intravenous antibiotic.*

psychotropic   *adj.* affecting mental perception and behavior: *Herbs and other plants having psychotropic properties are used today or have been* *used in the past in spiritual ceremonies by many different peoples. * The medication is a relatively mild psychotropic drug.*

puerile *adj.* immature, childish, and silly: *The style of these textbooks, if you can call it that, veers wildly between the puerile and the impenetrable.*

pugnacious *adj.* quarrelsome and combative; belligerent: *A pugnacious kid may be cute in the movies but not in the classroom.* Synonyms: **bellicose; truculent.**

pullulate *v.* **1** to produce young or sprout new shoots: *Left to their own devices, those critters would pullulate copiously.* **2** to swarm or infest: *Moments after he whacked that stump, the bees pullulated about his head.*
  pullulation *n.* a swarm or infestation: *What had at first been a couple of cute, furry animals became a pullulation of slightly terrifying creatures.*

punctilious *adj.* attentive to details of correct behavior, or exact and scrupulous: *His response was punctilious, but I imagine he must have been furious.*

punitive *adj.* serving as a punishment: *Such a labor-intensive approach to child-rearing is in many ways punitive to women who simply cannot spend that much time, and then blame themselves for not giving enough.*

punitively   *adv. You would hope they will not be punitively harassed when they are brought to halfway houses and reintegrated into society.*

purblind   *adj.* partially blind: *The only person to answer the ad was a very old, purblind, exparlormaid.*

purgative   *n.* something used to purge or clean out, especially the bowels: *The program acts like a purgative for your hard drive.*

purgatory   *n.* a place or condition in which someone must be for a time as a punishment; in Catholicism, a place or state in which the souls of the penitent suffer for a time for their transgressions: *It's hard to imagine a more perfect purgatory for someone so insistently impatient and brusque than being caught in the glacial machinations of a government bureaucracy.*

purview   *n.* **1** the scope or range of someone's or something's authority or control: *I can't really comment on these events—they're not within my purview.* **2** the range of someone's view: *It's best to limit your purview to what's straight ahead of you.*

putrescence   *n.* rot; foulness: *The putrescence of the hundreds of dead fish covering the shoreline kept everyone from the parks and beaches for weeks.*

putto   *n., pl.* **putti** a figure of an infant, male angel, or cherub in painting, sculpture, or decoration: *Above the entry were four putti holding a garland.* * *Postage stamps, her calendar, even the checks she uses have a picture of two putti on them.*

Q

CONFUSABLES

quietness/quietude *Quietness* is a lack of noise or sound (*An eerie quietness fell over the party.*); *quietude* is a condition of repose or peacefulness (*Their quietude was evident on the monks' faces.*).

---

qua *adv.* being of the particular quality or capacity of something; as: *I wasn't offended by the sex qua sex that the scandal revolved around.*

quagmire *n.* **1** a bog or marsh: *We made our way across the quagmire, soon picking up the trail to dry, higher ground.* **2** a difficult situation: *With the sudden death of our parents, we were left to pick our way through the quagmire of a lifetime's loose ends and confused finances.*

quarto *n.* a sheet of paper folded two times to make four leaves of eight pages, or a book with pages of medium size. See also **folio, octavo, quire**.

quaver *n. esp. British* an eighth note

quean *n.* a woman of ill repute, especially a prostitute: *Father said he would permit no quean in his house.*

querulous *adj.* finding fault and complaining about problems or inadequacies: *They filed a querulous, but unfortunately accurate, report.* * *Why are you so querulous lately?*
　　querulously *adv. The assistant querulously insisted the information in the file be updated immediately, even though the correct information was already in the computer.*

quiddity *n.* the essence of someone or something; its defining quality: *He quickly spotted my genius and encouraged me a lot in my quiddity, in my me-ness.*

quiescent *adj.* still, quiet, or at rest: *The fast climb left him gasping, but even as he became quiescent he was beginning to plan for tomorrow's hike.*

quietness/quietude see at Q CONFUSABLES

quietist *adj.* relating to a form of spiritual mysticism based on passive meditation: *Quakers had deep roots in mysticism and had been deeply quietist for much of the eighteenth century.*

quietism *n.* *Her artwork reflected her quietism and the Zenlike approach she took to most things.*

quietude *n.* a stillness or silentness: *There was a quietude about Bill that lent gravitas to everything he said.* See **quietness/quietude** at Q CONFUSABLES.

quire *n.* a set of twenty-four pieces of paper of the same size and weight; a twentieth of a ream: *The codex, a quire folded or sewn together, replaced the scroll, becoming the standard form of a manuscript.* See also **folio, octavo, quarto.**

quixotic *adj.* romantic and idealistic, yet impulsive and impractical; alike in character to Don Quixote: *My quixotic brother-in-law's noble intentions seem to cause him no end of problems.*

Don Quixote de la Mancha, from whose name *quixotic* derives, is the idealistically impractical hero of the eponymous romantic satire written by Miguel de Cervantes.

Book Words 2:
Terms Derived from Names of Books and Places in Books

Words describing books of the Bible (and would-be books of the Bible) join up with invented places described in novels to expand the Brobdingnagian range of the English language.

Apocalypse   *n.* any of the Jewish or Christian religious writings foretelling the end of the world, expecially the Book of Revelations in the New Testament.
> **apocalypse**   *n.* devastation and doom
> **apocalyptic**   *adj.* pertaining to the end of the world or its foretelling

Apocrypha   *pl., n.* fourteen books that were included in the Old Testament in very early versions of the Greek and Latin Bibles and are not considered canonical by Protestants; or early Christian writings rejected as part of the New Testament and not part of the Catholic or Protestant canons.
> **apocrypha**   *pl., n.* writings of questionable authorship or authenticity
> **apocryphal**   *adj.* false or of doubtful origin; factitious

Brobdingnag   *n.* the land where everything is gigantic, in *Gulliver's Travels* by Jonathan Swift

Brobdingnagian   *adj.* gigantic, enormous, or tremendous

Hagiographa   *pl., n.* the third of the three parts the Old Testament is divided into in the Jewish tradition, the first part being the Pentateuch and the second part Prophets.
   hagiography   *n.* a biography describing the lives of saints.

Laputa   *n.* a flying island where people devote themselves to impractical, visionary projects in *Gulliver's Travels* by Jonathan Swift.
   Laputan   *adj.* ridiculously impractical or devoted to visionary undertakings while neglecting more useful activities.

Lilliput   *n.* the land where everything is tiny in *Gulliver's Travels* by Jonathan Swift.
   Lilliputian   *adj.* very small in size, or trivial.

prelapsarian   *adj.* relating to the period before Adam and Eve's fall from grace.

quixotic   *adj.* romantic and idealistic, yet impulsive and impractical; alike in character to Don Quixote, the hero of the eponymous romantic satire written by Miguel de Cervantes.

Ruritania   *n.* an imaginary kingdom in the novel *The Prisoner of Zenda* by Anthony Hope.
   Ruritanian   *adj.* having to do with or having the characters of a mythical romantic place.

Utopia *n.* the island nation for which the fictional work written by Sir Thomas More is named.

　utopian *adj.* **1** perfect; ideal; relating to unrealistic plans of perfection; idealistic **2** pertaining to a utopia, an ideal society.

　utopia *n.* an ideal state or society where all social, political, and moral aspects of life have been perfected, or a fictional story about such a place.

quoin, coign *v.* to make or to finish with brick or stone the outside angles where the sides of a building meet: *These Italianate apartment buildings, built in the 1920s, are quoined, rusticated, and corniced.*

　quoin, coign *n.* an outside corner or angle of a building, or the corner-shaped brick or stone used to form this angle: *The quoins give a grander appearance to this otherwise unremarkable structure.*

quotidian *adj.* ordinary, everyday, humdrum: *My brother and I were involved in our quotidian grooming activities—knee-scrubbing, hair-combing, sock-straightening, that sort of thing.*

q.v. *abbreviation* Latin *quod vide*, "which see": *Further to my discussions in* Heacock's Dictionary of Disputables *(q.v.) I would like to mention several indisputable facts.*

R

CONFUSABLES

rack/wrack A *rack* is a shelf or frame for holding things, a medieval torture device, a bar with teeth that fit into the teeth of a gear, or a triangular frame used to place balls at the start of a game of pool; to *rack* means to torment (*Pain racked her every step.*), and it is used in the idiom *rack one's brains,* meaning to think very hard; *wrack* is used almost exclusively in the phrase *wrack and ruin* and means destruction and wreckage (*Troops quickly brought the region to wrack and ruin.*).

racket/racquet A *racket* is a lot of noise (*What's causing all that racket?*); a *racquet* or *racket* is a stringed paddle used in tennis, squash, badminton, etc. (*I need a new racquet—I threw out the last one after Hugh beat me last week.*).

raise/raze To *raise* means to lift up (*Raise your hand.*), increase (*Raise my salary.*), bring to maturity (*Cynthia raises Border collies.*), or put forward (*You raise a very good point.*); to *raze* means to tear down completely (*They razed a block of brownstones to make way for this office complex.*).

ravel/unravel Both words mean to untangle threads or to solve a mystery; *ravel* can also mean to tangle threads (*The kitten raveled my yarn.*).

ravish/ravage *Ravish* can mean to rape (*He'd bring the girls to the woods and then ravish them.*), or to fill someone with rapture and joy (*I was ravished by her beauty.*); *ravage* means to damage, devastate, or destroy a place (*Troops ravaged the village.*).

rebuff/repel/repulse To *rebuff* means to snub (*Our efforts to gain admission to the club were rebuffed.*); to *repel* means to drive back by force (*Government forces repelled the rebels.*), or to push away because of being disgusting (*His appearance repelled her.*); to *repulse* is to firmly turn away (*She repulsed his advances.*), or to cause to recoil (*Bloodshed repulses him.*).

rebut/refute To *rebut* something is to present the opposing view to it (*Defense witnesses rebutted the prosecutor's characterizations.*); to *refute* something is to prove it false (*Columbus refuted the notion that the world is flat.*).

reciprocal/mutual A *reciprocal* relationship is one in which something is done by the first party in return for something done by the second party (*Her kindness encouraged reciprocal behavior in others.*); a *mutual* activity or feeling is done or felt by each to or for the others, usually because of shared feelings (*Mutual respect is the cornerstone of a marriage.*); *mutual* can also mean common or joint (*a mutual friend*).

recurrence/reoccurrence A *recurrence* is a repeated happening (*the regular recurrence of hostilities in Ireland*); a *reoccurrence* is a single instance of repetition (*A reoccurrence of those symptoms could be serious.*).

refer/allude see **allude/refer** at A CONFUS-ABLES

regretful/regrettable also **regretable** If you are *regretful*, you feel sorrow because of circumstances beyond your control (*I was regretful about the closing of my favorite restaurant.*); a *regrettable* event or circumstance is one that causes or deserves regret (*It's regrettable that the restaurant has closed.*).

resin/rosin *Resin* is a clear or translucent substance used in varnishes, printing ink, plastics, and other products; *rosin* is one type of resin used to treat violin bows and to make varnish, soap, and other products.

revolve/rotate *Revolve* can mean to move in an orbit (*The earth revolves around the sun.*), or to spin on an axis (*She spun the top, watching it revolve in place.*); *rotate* means to spin on an axis (*The earth rotates once a day.*).

ripple/undulate see **undulate/ripple** at U CONFUSABLES

rococo/baroque see **baroque/rococo** at B CONFUSABLES

---

rabbit *v.* to discuss something unimportant; to ramble: *Not every author has the audacity to halt his narrative in midstream so he can rabbit on about groats.*

rack see at R CONFUSABLES

racket/racquet see at R CONFUSABLES

raise/raze see at R CONFUSABLES

raddle *v.* see **ruddle**

rancor *n.* deep, bitter feelings: *There seems to be no end to the rancor on either side in the endless troubles in Northern Ireland.*
  rancorous *adj. The court's ruling led to rancorous public debate across the country.*

rapacious *adj.* greedy; predatory: *The awful stereotype of the rapacious Jew was once a mainstay of popular fiction.*

  rapaciously *adv. The firm rapaciously subsumed its competitors.*

  rapaciousness *n. Decades of war, brutality, and the rapaciousness of corrupt leaders have left the people of Cambodia impoverished.*

  Synonym: **ravening**. See also **voracious**.

rapprochement *n.* establishment or reestablishment of friendly relations: *Everyone hopes this rapprochement will last, but after so many years of animosity, it will be difficult.* ∗ *A rapprochement between politicians and the body politic is sorely needed.*

raucous *adj.* **1** rowdy and disorderly; boisterous: *The director was fantastic at handling the raucous cast of seventh and eighth graders.* ∗ *the raucous trading floor of the stock exchange* **2** harsh or rough sounding: *a raucous laugh*

ravage see **ravish/ravage** at R CONFUSABLES

ravel see at R CONFUSABLES

ravening *adj.* greedy and predatory: *Tennyson spoke contemptuously of the ravening curiosity of scholars.* Synonym: **rapacious**. See also **ravenous**.

ravenous *adj.* **1** extremely hungry or eager to satisfy a need or desire, especially hunger: *Jesse is* *always ravenous—she's ready for a snack an hour after finishing a meal, yet she stays slim.* **2** greedy; rapacious: *His ravenous acquisitiveness finally caused his downfall.* Synonym: **voracious.** See also **ravening.**

ravenously *adv. I'm ravenously hungry.*

How Hungry Are You?

There are many ways to describe someone's appetite for or interest in food. Use these words abstemiously!

abstemious *adj.* consuming food and drink in moderation, or sparing.

bulimarexic *adj.* suffering from an eating disorder in which one alternately craves and is disgusted by food.

crapulous *adj.* showing signs of eating or drinking to great excess, or suffering from doing so.

epicure *n.* someone with a very refined taste for food and drink who greatly enjoys eating and drinking the finest.
  epicurean *adj.* very fancy and refined in taste.

gourmand *n.* someone who greatly enjoys food and drink, often to excess.

> **gourmet** *n.* someone who is very knowledge-able about and greatly enjoys good food.
>
> **ravenous** *adj.* extremely hungry, or eager to satisfy a need or desire, especially hunger.
>
> **voracious** *adj.* wanting or eating large amounts of food.

ravish see at R CONFUSABLES

raze see **raise/raze** at R CONFUSABLES

realpolitik, Realpolitik *n.* practical politics, especially politics based on power: *Ambassador Holbrooke's negotiation strategy has been called "Realpolitik with a human face."*

rebuff see at R CONFUSABLES

rebut see at R CONFUSABLES

recalcitrant *adj.* stubborn and difficult: *Ever tried to give a pill to a recalcitrant dog?*

recension *n.* a revision, or something resulting from revision: *Reinking's brilliant recension of Bob Fosse's dances in the revival of "Chicago" made the show a must-see.*

recherché *adj.* **1** rare, exotic, or obscure: *The books in the collection are publishing oddities and* *all quite recherché.* **2** artificial or pretentious: *I detest these recherché garden parties.* ∗ *His studied attempts at being casual and with-it came off as being completely recherché.* Compare **outré**.

recidivism   *n.* the tendency to fall back into earlier patterns of bad behavior, especially to revert to criminal ways: *Our justice system seems intent on seeking punishment but shows little inclination to try to stem the tide of recidivism that brings criminals back to prison again and again.*

>**recidivist**   *n.* someone who resumes his or her earlier patterns of bad behavior, especially criminal behavior: *Her study involved interviews with dozens of recidivists, their families, and the judges, social workers, and parole officers who dealt with them.*

>**recidivistic**   *adj. After more than a dozen years on the straight and narrow, he reverted to his earlier recidivistic behavior and was arrested shortly thereafter with a rock of crack cocaine in his pocket.*

reciprocal see at R CONFUSABLES

recondite   *adj.* little known, understood, or experienced: *Her research has led her to some of the more recondite examinations of third-century Celtic mysticism.*

recrimination   *n.* a countercharge of wrongdoing against an accuser: *Our arguments had become nasty, full of innuendos and recriminations.*

recriminatory *adj.* accusatory: *I'd followed the recipe to the letter, only to find a recriminatory pile of chopped onions still sitting on the counter.*

recrudescence *n.* a reoccurrence, especially of a disease or condition that has not been noticeable for some time: *These recrudescences bring to mind the feelings I had when the sores first appeared.*

rectilinear *adj.* having straight lines, or having the shape of a rectangle: *He smoothed the earthen walls until their surfaces were rectilinear.*

rectitude *n.* moral certainty, righteousness, or correctness: *Their belief in their own fair-mindedness displayed a rectitude that did not seem justified.*

recto *n.* the page of a manuscript meant to be read first, or a right-hand page in a book. Compare **verso**.

recumbent *adj.* reclining, lying down: *We found Paul recumbent on the living room floor, watching television.* Compare **prone**.

recurrence see at R CONFUSABLES

recuse *v.* to remove oneself as a judge to avoid an accusation of bias, or because one believes oneself to be biased: *It was a case from which Judge Rehnquist decided to recuse himself.*

redact   *v.* to edit or revise a piece of writing, or to outline a proposal: *Cynthia will redact the student activity book if it is necessary.*

   redactor   *n.* *The compilers will also be used as redactors in the later stages.*

   redaction   *n.* *This particular translation of the* Iliad *has been praised for the quality of the redaction as well as the accessibility of its language.*

reddle *v.* see **ruddle**

redolent   *adj.* **1** reminiscent or suggestive: *The design of the old abbey's gardens is redolent with history and gothic intrigue.* **2** smelling of; giving off a fragrance: *The funeral parlor was redolent with flowers.* * *The mouth-watering smell of redolent spices filled the house.*

redoubt   *n.* a fort or protective enclosure: *Paul and Tyler climbed up to see the view from the redoubt, and I waited for them in the tea shop off the castle's great hall.*

reductionism   *n.* the simplification of a complex issue, sometimes to the point of absurdly minimizing it: *This is not an exercise in reductionism, but you only have three months, so you do need to carefully focus your research.*

refer see **allude/refer** at A CONFUSABLES

refute see **rebut/refute** at R CONFUSABLES

regretable, **regrettable** see **regretful/regrettable** at R CONFUSABLES

regretful see at R CONFUSABLES

reify   *v.* to consider something abstract as a physical thing: *She could reify even the most obtuse subjects, like calculus and quantum physics.*
  reification   *n.* the act of making something abstract physical: *She cannot stop thinking of home, with its nocturnal sirens, its air-conditioning, its reification of the real.*

reliquary   *n.* a place or container in which relics are kept: *The hallway had become a reliquary and shrine of sorts to their ancestors. * A small, gold reliquary stood on the side altar.*

remonstrance   *n.* a protest or complaint: *She was offered lodging in a bungalow, which she felt was beneath her dignity, and her remonstrance led her to take up residence, along with her two children, in the railway station.*
  remonstration   *n. She paid no attention to our pleading and remonstrations, saying she would go regardless of what we said.*
  remonstrate   *v. We remonstrated with the guard, but to no avail.*

remunerate   *v.* to pay someone for work or a service: *Of course, we'll also remunerate you for the time it takes to research the project.*
  remuneration   *n. Remunerations offered by the company are competitive within the industry.*

renascent   *adj.* showing or having signs of renewed life and energy: *I had a sense of renascent possibility, the way you often do in springtime.*

reoccurrence   see **recurrence/reoccurrence** at R Confusables

reparation   *n.* the act of making amends, especially for wrongdoing; redress: *The oldest daughter's friends caused the damage to the pool filter and they will make reparation.*
   reparations   *pl. n.* compensation for a loss made by those responsible: *The company will have to pay the court-ordered reparations.* * *payment of war reparations*

repel   see **rebuff/repel/repulse** at R Confusables

replete   *adj.* full of, containing many of, or overflowing with: *The roof was replete with gutters that drained into a tank, forcing water away from the entrance.*

reprobate   *n.* a person without principles: *The candidate, a well-known reprobate, nevertheless easily won the loyally Tory constituency.*
   reprobate   *adj. I try to avoid that reprobate gambler who hangs out in front of the grocery.*

repudiate   *v.* to deny, reject, or refuse to acknowledge someone or something: *By repudiating the party's candidate for the governorship, the mayor risks his own political future for short-term gain.*

repugnant *adj.* very disagreeable, offensive, or distasteful: *Can you continue to admire someone's business acumen in the face of such repugnant prejudice? * I thought her behavior was morally repugnant.*

repulse see **rebuff/repel/repulse** at R CONFUSABLES

resin see at R CONFUSABLES

restive *adj.* impatient with delay or criticism, or stubborn and resistant about doing something: *We'd been waiting to take off for almost an hour, and the passengers were becoming restive.*

resuscitate *v.* **1** to revive, bring back, or give new life to: *Overcrowding in the elementary schools resuscitated the previously defeated plan to add a new wing at the middle school and move all sixth graders there.* **2** to cause a person whose lungs and heart have stopped working to begin breathing again: *The EMT resuscitated the child.*

retrogress *v.* to return to a previous condition: *After decades of steadily improving relations, it took just one small incident for things to retrogress completely.*
    retrogression *n. In the civil-rights era, the words "Little Rock" became associated with retrogression in the field of race relations.*

revenant *n.* someone who returns, specifically a ghost or spirit of someone formerly living: *There's* *no need to fear a ghost—what power, after all, does a revenant have beyond simply appearing?* Compare **apparition**.

revolve see at R CONFUSABLES

rhadamanthine, Rhadamanthine *adj.* strict and rigorously just: *Critics pretend to be rhadamanthine in their pronunciamentos, but they are just as biased and self-centered as anyone else.*

rhapsodic, rhapsodical *adj.* expressed with passion and enthusiasm: *Barnes's rhapsodic review was the only positive notice the show got.*
   rhapsodically, rhapsodic *adv. He sings rhapsodically, with great depth and emotion.* ∗ *My little brother waxed rhapsodic over our grandma's illuminated painting of the Last Supper.*

rhapsody *n.* ecstasy; intense delight: *He thought he'd undertaken this pilgrimage only with hope, but now he realized he'd expected rhapsody and was disappointed.*

rhetoric *n.* **1** the act or skill of writing or speaking effectively: *a master of rhetoric* **2** language suitable for a particular audience: *legal rhetoric*
   rhetorical *adj.* said only for effect: *I didn't think you wanted an answer—it sounded like a rhetorical question to me.*
   rhetorically *adv. I was speaking rhetorically.*

rictus *n.* a gaping opening of the mouth, usually in surprise or fear: *He bent his knees and spread his arms, his mouth stretched in a rictus of grinning terror.*

rile *v.* to irritate, annoy, or upset: *The decision of the town to allow diversion of the creek has riled environmentalists, who have now filed suit.* Synonym: **roil**.

ripple see **undulate/ripple** at U CONFUSABLES

risible *adj.* causing laughter; ludicrous; laughable: *Prohibition was, in the end, a risible regulatory effort.*
  risibly *adj. risibly inadequate safeguards*

rivalrous *adj.* marked by rivalry or competition: *In rivalrous camaraderie, the climbers spent the evening swapping stories and insults.*

rococo see **baroque/rococo** at B CONFUSABLES

roil *v.* to cause someone or something to become disturbed, irritated, or upset: *The targeted toll increases are sure to roil suburban commuters.* Synonym: **rile**.

rosin see **resin/rosin** at R CONFUSABLES

rotate see **revolve/rotate** at R CONFUSABLES

roundelay *n.* a song or poem with a regular refrain or repeated phrase: *The chorus will perform a roundelay composed by one of the senior music students.*

The Name of a Song

Interesting terminology can be employed when discussing musical forms and styles. There's even an excellent word for naming your do-re-mi's. Different types of songs may have a specific form or convey a particular mood. Do you know whether you're listening to a ballad or a lament?

air *n.* a song, especially an art song, or the main melody in a song sung in parts.

anthem *n.* a song praising God, or a song of patriotic devotion.

antiphon *n.* a verse chanted or sung in two alternating parts, usually a statement and response, especially as part of religious worship.

art song *n.* a song having a poetic text and usually sung in recital.

ballad *n.* a simple romantic or sentimental song.

carol *n.* a Christmas song.

chanson   *n.* a song, usually one sung in French, especially a cabaret song.

dirge   *n.* a song of mourning, especially a funeral song.

hymn   *n.* a song of glorification or praise, especially to God.

lament   *n.* a song of sorrow or mourning, or a dirge.

lied   *n.* a lyrical song, usually one sung in German, or a German art song.

madrigal   *n.* a love poem sung a cappella in counterpoint by four to six voices.

paean   *n.* a song or other expression of praise or triumph.

roundelay   *n.* a song or poem with a regular refrain or repeated phrase.

solfège, solfeggio   *n.* the use of the syllables *do, re, me, fa, so, la, ti, do* in singing exercises.

---

rubric   *n.* a category, classification, heading, or title: *To conflate musicians as diverse as John Williams and Philip Glass under the rubric of "twentieth-century composers" seems misleading, to say the least.*

ruddle, reddle, raddle   *v.* to color with red ochre, or to cause to become a reddish color: *I felt my face ruddle in embarrassment.*
　　ruddled   *adj.* having a reddish color: *I poured the ruddled grapefruit juice into the two glasses.*

rufous   *adj.* red or reddish: *Her rufous hair shone lustrously against her alabaster skin.*

ruminate   *v.* to think carefully and deliberately: *She ruminated for several days before turning down his proposal.*
　　rumination   *n.* meditation; thought and consideration: *I don't see why a lengthy rumination should be needed.*

Ruritanian   *adj.* having to do with or having the characteristics of a mythical romantic place: *Kate envisioned New York as some Ruritanian realm in which love is around every corner.*

Ruritania, from which the adjective "Ruritanian" derives, is an imaginary kingdom in the novel *The Prisoner of Zenda* by Anthony Hope.

---

rusticate   *v.* **1** to go to a rural place to visit or live: *After the hurly-burly of the financial world, Walter was not sure he'd be able to successfully rusticate himself.* **2** to force someone to move to the country: *As a small boy, Frank was removed from his Bronx* *environs and rusticated on his uncle's farm in Ireland.* **3** to build a structure with noticeable, beveled points in the masonry: *His houses are noted for their rusticated facades.*

S

CONFUSABLES

sac/sack A *sac* is a pouch in or on an animal or plant, often one that holds liquid (*the testicular sac*), or in baseball slang, a sacrifice; a *sack* is a bag (*a grocery sack*), a loose-fitting dress (*She often wears a sack dress and sandals in the summer.*), a bed (*Let's hit the sack.*) or in baseball slang, a base (*His foot never touched the sack.*).

sardonic/sarcastic Something *sardonic* is mocking, derisive, or cynical (*She made some sardonic comment about government officials looking to get a little on the side.*); *sarcastic* means expressing ridicule or openly taunting (*On seeing she had nowhere to go, her sarcastic comment was, "I'm delighted to be here."*).

scull/skull A *scull* is an oar or a racing rowboat (*Laura could be found in the early morn-*

ings rowing a scull down the Potomac.); a *skull* is the bones of the head.

seasonable/seasonal *Seasonable* means appropriate to the season (*seasonable weather*); *seasonal* means controlled by or having to do with the season (*a seasonal change in unemployment*).

sense/sensibility *Sense* is judgment, intelligence, or mental capability (*Sometimes you act like you have no sense at all.*); *sensibility* is susceptibility, sensitivity, or the ability to feel things (*His sensibilities were offended by the so-called artwork.*).

sensual/sensuous *Sensual* means having to do with the satisfaction of physical desire and fleshly appetites (*Her sensual needs were not being met.*); *sensuous* means having to do with the satisfaction of the esthetic senses (*The sensuous play of the light on the water pleased him.*).

signal/singular *Signal*, as an adjective, means unusually good or unusually bad (*Winning this award is a signal accomplishment.*); *singular* means unique and exceptional (*DiMaggio's consecutive-game hitting streak was a singular accomplishment.*).

site/cite see **cite/site** at C CONFUSABLES

slander/libel see **libel/slander** at L Confusables

sprain/strain A *sprain* is the result of a sudden, violent wrenching of muscles or ligaments (*sprain an ankle*); a *strain* is an
overtaxation of muscles or ligaments caused
by using them either for too long or to do too
much (*strain your back carrying a heavy
suitcase*).

stalactite/stalagmite A *stalactite* is a conical
mineral formation attached to a cave's ceiling;
a *stalagmite* is a conical mineral formation
standing on a cave's floor.

stationary/stationery A *stationary* object is
not moving; *stationery* is writing material.

stigma/stigmata A *stigma* is a mark, stain, or
spot, either literal or figurative (*It's hard to
believe there was once an enormous stigma
attached to being homosexual.*); *stigmata*,
which is one of the plural forms of *stigma*, is
most often used to mean marks like those on
Christ's crucified body (*a holy shroud showing
the stigmata*).

strategy/tactics A *strategy* is a large-scale
plan of action (*Walter's strategy was simple—
the team should win every game, all year, to
assure itself a spot in the playoffs.*); *tactics* are
plans for each specific part of an overall plan

(*A pitcher uses different tactics when there are runners on base from when the bases are empty.*).

supine/prone see **prone/supine** at P CONFUS-ABLES

sympathy/empathy see **empathy/sympathy** at E CONFUSABLES

---

sac see at S CONFUSABLES

saccharine *adj.* **1** having a distinctly sweet taste: *a saccharine drink* **2** overly sweet or sentimental; ingratiating: *Every Christmas a steady stream of saccharine movies is shown on TV.*

sack see **sac/sack** at S CONFUSABLES

sacralize *v.* to make sacred or holy: *Once he established his leadership of the cult, he tried to sacralize his sexual desires.*
   sacralization *n. He used the language of sacralization to give a tone of moral purity to his purely political ambitions.*

sagacity *n.* discernment and sound judgment: *I was very impressed during the interview by the sagacity of the Dalai Lama.*

sage *n.* a wise and judicious person: *The advisory council was created so the organization wouldn't lose the experience and expertise of these sages, who* *are no longer involved in the program on a regular basis.*

   sage   *adj.* *Over the years, my mother gave me some very sage advice.*

salacious   *adj.* lecherous or obscene; sexually stimulating: *The salacious stories about the governor contained more than mere innuendo.*

   salaciousness   *n.* *The dean's salaciousness was out of order.*

salubrious   *adj.* promoting health and wellness: *If the tale inspires news addicts to fall into the many-layered, humanizing, fathoming raptures of literature, nothing could be more salubrious.*

salutary   *adj.* having a positive effect, or causing health and well-being: *Looking back on this stupid, hysterical behavior, we hope others will be able to at least draw a salutary lesson from it. * The salutary effects of these waters have not been scientifically proven, but people have come here for centuries in order to drink and bathe.*

sanctimonious   *adj.* pretending piety, devotion, or righteousness: *She's fawning and sanctimonious, and I don't trust her. * The stories, written by a monk, never sound sanctimonious or trite.*

   sanctimony   *n.* *The lies and sanctimony have got to stop.*

sangfroid   *n.* calmness and composure: *She hadn't expected her parents to react with such sangfroid* *when she told then she'd taken a job halfway across the country.*

sanguinary   *adj.* bloody or bloodthirsty: Saving Private Ryan *must be one of the most sanguinary Hollywood flicks ever made.*

sanguine   *adj.* **1** hopeful and cheerfully optimistic: *The more sanguine computer users accept the vagaries of systems that suddenly insist a piece of hardware it was telephoning with only minutes before doesn't exist.* **2** sanguinary: *Rescuers came upon the sanguine aftermath of the wreck.*

sarcastic see **sardonic/sarcastic** at S Confusables

sardonic see at S Confusables

sartorial   *adj.* relating to tailoring or tailored clothing: *The grandsons tried to turn the old man's once successful store into a sartorial empire and lost everything.* * *I'm afraid his manners did not match his sartorial elegance.*

saturnine   *adj.* having a gloomy, sullen disposition: *He's a dark, saturnine man in his late forties.*

saurian   *n.* a suborder of reptiles that includes lizards and some extinct creatures, such as dinosaurs and ichthyosaurs: *It looked like a saurian, but it scrambled into the underbrush before he could get a good enough look to be sure.*

saurian *adj.* like a lizard or a dinosaur: *A clamor rose from the street, a great saurian roar of fire engine sirens.*

savor *n.* a certain quality: *The trappings of the Christmas holidays seems often to have more the savor of ancient European pagan celebrations than the religiosity of later Christian observance.*

scant *v.* to give little credence or importance to: *Genna doesn't scant the role of antibodies in fighting the virus, but her work shows that antibodies may prove to be an even more powerful weapon.*

scapular *n.* two pieces of cloth, worn on the front and back under clothing and tied with string, that some Roman Catholics wear to signify their devotion or to show their membership in a particular order: *His mother always wore a scapular.*

schadenfreude *n.* joy taken from the problems and troubles of others: *The more accomplished an athlete becomes, the greater the role of schadenfreude in his emotional life.*

scintillant *adj.* sparkling; scintillating: *The colored glass in the front windows had a scintillant quality.*

scion *n.* a child or descendant, especially one from a wealthy or important family: *She used to get love letters from the scion of the Ford family.*

sclerotic *adj.* characterized by a hardening of tissue, especially of an artery, or immobile or unchanging: *Poland's sclerotic Communist rule gave way to a democratic system.*

scourge *n.* **1** someone or something that causes affliction: *A vaccine has saved millions from the scourge of polio.* **2** someone who criticizes or punishes: *She's the scourge of every attempt to change policy on social issues.*

scull see at S CONFUSABLES

scumble *v.* to soften or obscure colors or lines: *She starts with vivid, primary colors, then scumbles them with a translucent wash.*
  scumble *n. A sentimental scumble masks his observations, making them less pointed and less worth reading.*

seasonable/seasonal see at S CONFUSABLES

sectarian *adj.* supporting or pertaining to a particular group or the beliefs of a particular group: *Northern Ireland is not the only place with a long history of sectarian strife.* * *The poll showed clear sectarian divisions.*

secularize *v.* to make something that is religious nonreligious or worldly: *The values celebrated in these depictions of Christmas are material values—a secularized celebration.*

sedition *n.* the act of encouraging others to overthrow or refuse to obey the government: *Charged with sedition and treason, he felt he had little choice but to seek asylum overseas.*

    seditious *adj. Left-wing agitators cheered his seditious speeches, hoping they would at last bring about the long-awaited revolution.*

seigneurial *adj.* behaving like or having the manner of a person of prestige, rank, or authority: *O'Connor's seigneurial airs proved fodder for more than a few jokes at his expense this evening.*

self-deprecating *adj.* showing a good-natured lack of self-importance, especially by making jokes at one's own expense or belittling one's own achievements: *Dole's self-deprecating speech included references to his electoral defeat as "something that happened to me last November."* See also **deprecate**.

semibreve *n. esp. British* a whole note

semiotics, semeiotics *n.* the study of signs and symbols; a theory of signs and symbols used in language: *Success in debate requires preparation, a quick wit, an understanding of semiotics, and a good voice.*

    semiotician, semeiotician *n. A successful politician is a capable semiotician, evoking those symbols that represent the beliefs the populace holds most dear.*

semiquaver   *n. esp. British* a sixteenth note

senesce   *v.* to grow old; age: *The leaves and needles of evergreens do senesce and fall from the tree— when depends on the species, but never all of them at one time.*

>   **senescent**   *adj.* aging: *Their senescent car is back in the shop.*

>   **senescence**   *n.* an aging state; the state or condition of becoming older: *There is a limit to the number of times a cell can divide, then it lapses into senescence.*

sense   see at S CONFUSABLES

sensibility   see **sense/sensibility** at S CONFUSABLES

sensual/sensuous   see at S CONFUSABLES

sentient   *adj.* perceived by or through the senses, or able to perceive this way; conscious: *A sentient being would not stand living in such squalor.*

sepulcher, sepulchre   *n.* a tomb or burial place: *Somberly, they approached the sepulcher, heads bowed and hearts heavy.*

>   **sepulchral**   *adj.* suitable for a funeral; funereal: *We were having a great time, but the others at the party had a sepulchral look on their faces as they spoke in whispers.*

seraglio   *n.* the women's part of a Muslim house; a harem: *From the seraglio stepped a veiled woman.*

seraphic, seraphical *adj.* angelic; like the sera-phim: *He's a beautiful, round-faced little boy with wide, dark-brown eyes and a seraphic smile.*

seraphim *n.* the highest of the nine orders of angels
    seraphim *n., pl.* **seraphim,** also **seraph** *n., pl.* **seraphs** an angel of the highest order. See THE CELESTIAL HIERARCHY at **angel.**

sere *adj.* dried-out: *Out west, everything was dif-ferent—the sky was brighter, and the earth was sere.*

serendipity *n.* good luck in experiencing good things accidentally: *I'd given up all hope of finding someone like you, so our meeting like this was just serendipity.*
    serendipitous *adj.* lucky: *The book's organiza-tion is serendipitous, dependent on where and when it was written rather than on any advance planning.*

serried *adj.* placed or made to stand closely to-gether: *I loved going to the supermarket, where I would inspect the serried ranks of ketchup bottles, toilet paper rolls, and loaves of bread.*

servile *adj.* slavishly submissive and obedient, or relating to servitude: *Why would you expect your waiter to be servile?* * *servile tasks*

sesqui-   *prefix* one and a half: *The club celebrated its sesquicentennial.* ∗ *He claims to be sesquilingual—he speaks one-and-a-half languages.*

shibboleth   *n.* a peculiarity held by a person or by a group of people: *Before the coffin was closed, the family gathered beside it to say their good-byes and leave inside some small mementos—a shibboleth frowned on by other of their relations.*

sibilant   *n.* a consonant sound that is a soft hiss, such as the "s" in "pleasure": *An excess of sibilants slide past the retainer she wears to straighten her teeth.*
   sibilant   *adj.* hissing: *Sibilant radiators woke us at dawn.*

sibyl   *n.* a woman who can tell the future: *What sibyl was this, who predicted my downfall while I was still at the height of success?*
   sibylline   *adj. The first chapter contained one of her most sibylline passages, presaging her characters' actions in ways that made them seem preordained.*

In the ancient world, a sibyl was a prophetess. According to classical mythology, there were thought to be ten sibyls located in separate parts of the world.

sidereal *adj.* relating to the stars: *The tent's window flap was open, so we could watch the vast sidereal plane sliding past as we drifted off to sleep.*

signal see at S Confusables

silvan *adj.* See **sylvan**

similitude *n.* the resemblance or similarity one thing has to another, or the sameness of related things: *The similitude of U.S. currency is strange and confusing to most Europeans.*

simulacrum *n., pl.* **simulacra** an image or superficial likeness of something: *Today most law schools offer real-world experience in addition to the simulacra of moot court and situational role-plays.*

singular *adj.* exceptional, unusual, or like no others: *For three decades, Ali was a singular presence in professional sports.* See **signal/singular** at S Confusables

site see **cite/site** at C Confusables

skein *n.* **1** a coil of thread or hair: *She picked up the skein of yarn.* **2** a flock of birds: *A skein of geese were flapping northwards.* **3** a group or series of events: *The Yankees' skein of losses at the start of the season had fans worried.*

skull see **scull/skull** at S Confusables

slander see **libel/slander** at L Confusables

slurry *n.* a thin mixture of a liquid, usually water, with a fine, insoluble substance, such as clay, plaster, or charcoal: *The sudden rain turned the coals in the barbecue into a sad slurry.*

sobriquet *n.* a nickname: *He wouldn't tell me how he'd picked up the sobriquet "Lionel."*

solecism *n.* **1** an instance of using language incorrectly or ungrammatically: *His speech was peppered with solecisms—using "done" for "did" and "be" for "is"—that made me think he was trying too hard to prove he's just one of the guys.* **2** a mistake or error; a faux pas: *The couple had committed the solecism of ordering an appetizer in addition to the huge and unfinishable taco salad.*

solfège, solfeggio *n.* the use of the syllables *do, re, me, fa, so, la, ti, do* in singing exercises: *The telephone dial tone is the very solfège of modern life.*

solipsism *n.* **1** the belief that one can never know anything beyond what one personally experiences, and that one's self is the only existing thing: *Directors whose movies are based solely on other movies, rather than on life itself, often indulge in unbearable solipsism.* **2** overindulgence in one's own needs, feelings, and ideas: *Solipsism is not a function of his being old and infirm—he's always been totally self-absorbed.*

  solipsistic *adj.* excessively self-centered and self-absorbed; egotistical: *I broke up with him be-*

*cause I couldn't take his solipsistic self-promotion
and competitiveness anymore.*

souk   *n.* an open-air Arab marketplace in a city:
*Gossips in the souk said he had been unfaithful to
his wife.*

specious   *adj.* seemingly right but actually without
merit: *The escalation of U.S. involvement in Viet-
nam was based on the specious premise of the Dom-
ino Theory.* Compare **spurious**.

spindrift, spoondrift   *n.* the spray blown by wind
into the air from the surface of the sea: *A fine mist
of spindrift coating Tyler's hair glistened in the sun.*

splenetic   *adj.* bad-tempered, irritable, and spite-
ful: *He's bitchy and splenetic because he's over-
worked and overtired.*

spoliation   *n.* **1** the act of damaging, despoiling, or
plundering: *This is an investigation into a murder
committed by two children, and an examination of
the spoliation of innocence.* **2** the illegal destruction
or alteration of a document: *He admitted to the
spoliation of the ownership papers.*

sprain see at S CONFUSABLES

spurious   *adj.* not as claimed; not real or not genuine: *A hundred years ago, scientists posited a spurious link between periodontal disease and arthritis.*
Compare **specious**.

stalactite/stalagmite see at S CONFUSABLES

stationary/stationery see at S CONFUSABLES

stele, stela   *n., pl.* **steles, stelae** an upright stone marker or monument with a design or inscription engraved on it: *The style of engraving on these stelae indicate the site may be older than archeologists had thought.*

stentorian   *adj.* very loud: *He turned on the shower and began singing in the voice of a stentorian frog.*

stigma/stigmata see at S CONFUSABLES

stodgy   *adj.* conventional, traditional, or old-fashioned: *The new editor has given the stodgy newsletter a thorough overhaul, from its typeface to its journalistic style.*

stoicism   *n.* indifference to emotion, pleasure, and pain: *Stoicism will prove an inadequate refuge from fear.*

stolid   *adj.* unemotional, or appearing to have no feelings: *Clarence was a stolid, unhurrying presence in the office.*

strain see **sprain/strain** at S CONFUSABLES

strategy see at S CONFUSABLES

striated *adj.* having ridges or farrows: *I received a beautiful, striated crystal vase.*

stricture *n.* a restriction or limitation: *Because of baseball's arcane strictures, a prospective purchaser of a team must agree to terms before seeing the team's books.*

stultifying *adj.* foolish, or dull, sluggish, and apathetic: *The job was repetitious, boring, stultifying in the extreme.*
   stultifyingly *adv. The presentation was stultifyingly academic.*

stygian, **Stygian** *adj.* dark and gloomy, or hellish; pertaining to the river Styx: *Steve was deep in a Stygian funk. * We traveled through underground tunnels, stygian tubes deep in the bowels of the city.*

Stygian originally referred to the river Styx. In Greek mythology, the Styx is the river in Hades over which the souls of the dead are ferried.

---

subordinate *adj.* secondary to or less important than something else: *After decades in charge, it's not easy taking on a subordinate role.*
   subordination *n. As a scientist, he was irritated by the subordination of his research to the marketplace orientation of the company, but as a part-owner, he stood to gain financially.*
   subordinate *v.* to make something less important or secondary to something else: *She subordi-*

nates her needs to those of her husband in ways that are inspiring and pathetic in equal measure.

subornation *n.* the persuasion of someone to do something unlawful, especially to lie under oath: *Today's paper says the testimony of three witnesses is suspect because of alleged subornation of perjury by the mob.*
  suborn *v. Her attorney was accused of suborning witnesses.*

subvert *v.* to undermine or overthrow: *Veeck loved to subvert the baseball establishment, running promotions and stunts that made it clear he did not take the game too seriously.*

succubus *n., pl.* **succubi** an evil female spirit or devil: *As the relationship became increasingly nightmarish, he started to think of her overtures as those of a succubus, trying to gain his soul with sex.* Compare **incubus**.

In medieval times, a succubus was thought to be a devil in the form of a woman, who had sex with a sleeping man.

sufflate *v.* to inflate: *The wind sufflated the plastic bag, lofting it above the rooftops and sending it on a perilous journey.*
  sufflation *n.* inflation: *He was assaulted by emptiness and fear, plunged into a negative moment*

of being, feeling as though sufflation were being emptied from him.

sui generis *adj.* without compare; unique: *He's known for being the son of a former president and the brother of a governor, but on this occasion he was just himself, sui generis, acting as a man.*

supercilious *adj.* showing contempt and disdain: *The young model had the usual supercilious stare so strangely popular in mass market advertisements.*

supernumerary *n.* someone or something extra: *When he retired, her father felt superfluous, a supernumerary without a clear identity or position in the world at large.*

supine *adj.* lying face up, on one's back: *He was on the bed, supine, with a fan blowing over him, trying to sleep on this hot, hot night.* See **prone/ supine** at P CONFUSABLES. Antonym: **prone**.

suppliant *n.* a petitioner; someone who makes an earnest request; a supplicant: *Several lawyers with their clients entered the courtroom—suppliants waiting to hear if their petitions had been granted.*
   suppliant *adj. The team's suppliant note to the review committee won them a chance to present their project proposal.*

supplicate *v.* to request humbly or earnestly, beg, or seek favor from a god or authority: *We suppli-*

cate the fashion gods by glorifying an unnatural thinness.

supra- *prefix* over, above, or outside of: *Many of the world's supranational institutions, such as the International Court of Justice and the World Health Organization, were formed under the auspices of the U.N.*

surfeit *n.* a sufficient or overabundant amount: *We've had a surfeit of tragedies and felt life now owed us a little more ease.*
   surfeit *v. The whole of Africa seems surfeited with poverty and disease and disaster.*

surmount *v.* to conquer or overcome: *You will have to surmount the review committee's bias toward the candidate whose work they are already familiar with.*
   surmountable *adj. a surmountable difficulty*

susurrate *v.* to make a low, murmuring sound: *We were lulled to sleep by the babbling brook running past our window, susurrating as it flowed by.*
   susurration *n.* a quiet, rustling sound: *They were bathed in the susurrations of the wind on the water.*

sybarite *n.* someone who indulges in pleasure and luxury: *Silverman is a sybarite who refuses to kneel before the mundane demands of the workaday world.*
   sybaritic *adj. The design of the royal gardens re-*

flected the sybaritic aesthetic of prerevolutionary France.

sycophantic *adj*. in a fawning or obsequiously flattering manner: *They thanked us in such sycophantic terms that I began to doubt their sincerity.*

sylph *n*. a thin, graceful young woman: *Spirited sylphs swanned across the stage, adding a decorative beauty that enhanced the music.*

sylvan, silvan *adj*. characteristic of, located in, or appearing like woods or forests: *We sat in the sylvan shade, enjoying a respite from the morning's hike.*
    sylvan *n*. someone who lives in or spends time in the woods: *These creatures are natural sylvans who have begun to forage in the encroaching suburban neighborhoods.*

symmetrical, symmetric *adj*. having on either side of a central dividing line elements of corresponding form, size, and position: *The main room of the lodge had a symmetrical design, with seating arranged by the fireplaces at either end.* Antonym: **asymmetrical.**

sympathy see **empathy/sympathy** at E Confusables

synchrony *n*. simultaneous occurrence: *Even newborns move in synchrony with the cadence of speech.*

syncopated *adj.* having a rhythm that stresses a beat that is not the usually stressed beat: *The women dance across the courtyard, advancing like a syncopated army.*

synecdoche *n.* a figure of speech in which the word for an individual, part, or substance is used instead of the word for a group, whole, or manufactured thing, or the word for a group, etc., is used for the individual: *The senator kept using a synecdoche, saying "soldier" when he meant "the army."*

synergy *n.* the combination or cooperation of separate forces, energies, or strengths, resulting in something more powerful or effective: *The boss hopes your analytic mind and my intuitive approach will get some synergy going.*
   synergistic *adj.* powerful because of being in combination: *Team teaching can have a synergistic effect in the classroom.*
   synergistically *adv.* *My own memories and reflections combined synergistically with the research I carried out in the library.*

synoptic *adj.* general, broad, or comprehensive: *Boorstin's latest book offers nothing less than a synoptic overview of Western religious and philosophical thought.*

systemic *adj.* involving an entire system, or affecting the entire body: *Changing procedures in one area won't help—the problems at the warehouse are systemic.* * *The research has not clearly impli-*

cated silicone breast implants in any systemic abnormalities.

syzygy *n.* the positioning in almost a straight line of three astronomical bodies, as the sun, the moon, and the earth during an eclipse

T

CONFUSABLES

tasty/tasteful If something is *tasty* it is flavorful (*a tasty meal*) or attractive and interesting (*some tasty gossip about showbiz figures*); *tasteful* means exhibiting good esthetic judgment (*a tasteful outfit*).

thrash/thresh *Thrash* means to beat or flog a person (*My dad could thrash your dad.*), or to defeat or trounce an opponent (*The Yankees thrashed the Indians, 21–1.*); *thresh* means to separate seeds or grain from straw or chaff.

tortuous/torturous *Tortuous* means winding or twisted (*a tortuous mountain road*), or deceitful and tricky (*What tortuous leadership brought us to this pass?*); *torturous* means painful (*I spent a torturous morning in one of those interminable meetings our department seems to specialize in.*).

transpire/happen If something *transpires*, it becomes known despite efforts to keep it secret (*Our carefully prepared plans transpired, and we lost the element of surprise.*); *transpire* is also used synonymously with *happen* to mean occur.

treachery/treason *Treachery* is betrayal of a confidence (*Your treachery cost me my boyfriend.*); *treason* is betrayal of a country (*Selling secrets to foreign agents is an act of treason.*).

troop/troupe A *troop* is a group of people (*a Boy Scout troop*); a *troupe* is a group of actors, singers, or dancers (*The Bolshoi troupe is staying at the Savoy Hotel.*)

---

tabula rasa *n.* a blank slate; a pure and unsullied condition, especially of the mind: *If you completely discount the role of genetics, you could consider the human mind as a tabula rasa at birth, awaiting the imprint of parents and society.*

tactics see **strategy/tactics** at S CONFUSABLES

tactile *adj.* having to do with the sense of touch: *He needs to touch everything—he even turns viewing a painting into a tactile exploration.*

talus *n.* **1** *pl.* **taluses** a slope on a mountainside formed by rock debris: *We scrambled up the talus of the mesa.* **2** *pl.* **tali** the ankle, or the tarsal bone which bears the weight in the ankle: *Marj's accident shattered her talus, leaving her unable to walk.*

tasty/tasteful see at T CONFUSABLES

tatterdemalion *n.* a person wearing tattered, ragged clothing: *Here beneath the bridge lives a group of tatterdemalions, warm in their corrugated brown boxes.*
  tatterdemalion *adj.* tattered, or ragged: *The cabin turned out to be a tiny dark shack with broken windows and tatterdemalion furnishings.*

tatty *adj.* cheap and shabby: *The water was shut off because the plumbing repairs weren't finished, so we spent the night a tatty motel.*

taxonomy *n.* a classification or division into ordered groups; the system by which something is classified or ordered: *Taxonomies are not immutable, whether you see astrophysics as a part of physics, of astronomy, or of both depends on the theory of classification you use.*

tegument *n.* See at **integument**.

telamon *n., pl.* **telamones** a supporting column sculpted in the form of a male figure. Synonym: **atlas**. Compare **caryatid**.

teleology *n.* the belief or doctrine that there is an ultimate, underlying design that phenomena must follow: *The company's teleology seems to be that* *sports serves as a powerful community bond in a society that is increasingly fragmented by an over-abundance of entertainment choices.*

temerity *n.* boldness, disregard of danger: *In nature, temerity has obvious payoffs: territory, dominance, food, and a mate.* Antonym: **timidity**.

tensile *adj.* having the maximum strength possible for its type: *Her tensile-tough compositions are enhanced by her sentimental use of color and light.*

tenuous *adj.* weak or vague; without a firm basis: *Now that he's out of jail, Tyson is making tenuous comments about another comeback.*

termagant *n.* a quarrelsome, violent woman; a shrew: *Some views of Joan of Arc paint her as a terrifying termagant rather than a saint.* Synonym: **virago.**

In medieval morality plays, Termagant is an imaginary deity thought by European Christians to be worshiped by Muslims and portrayed as an overbearing character.

terpsichorean *adj.* having to do with dance: *Terpsichorean afficionados are deploring what they see as a weakening of standards brought about by modern dance.*

> **terpsichorean** *n.* a dancer: *the renowned terpsichorean, Suzanne Farrell*
> (See note next page)

In classical mythology, Terpsichore, from whose name "terpsichorean" derives, was the Muse of dance.

tessera *n., pl.* **tesserae** a small square used in making mosaics: *If one of the tesserae comes out, the others around it are more likely to loosen.*

tetralogy *n.* a series of four connected works, such as stories or operas: *His towering tetralogy of life in a distant galaxy in the thirty-second century has met with great critical acclaim.*

thalassic *adj.* having to do with inland seas: *These thalassic spas have been attracting visitors for thousands of years.*

Thanatos *n.* an impulse or inclination toward death; a death instinct: *The gunman seemed to have become caught up in Thanatos and paranoia.*
    thanatophiliac *n.* someone with an abnormal fear of death: *You need to get out and do things and not be constantly worrying, or you'll wind up locking yourself up at home like my thanatophiliac neighbor.*
    thanatophobia *n.* an abnormal fear of death.

In classical mythology, Thanatos is the personification of death.

thaumatology   *n.* the study of wonders or miracles: *There were rumors of mystical visions, reports that touched on the subject of thaumatology.*

thaumaturge   *n.* a practitioner of miracles, or a magician: *He had renown in his home country as something of a thaumaturge, not that anyone here would care.*

   thaumaturgy   *n.* magic: *She was accused of thaumaturgy by local clerics who couldn't understand how such healing could have occurred.*

theocracy   *n.* a government in which decisions are the result of divine guidance: *The Iranian theocracy dictates many aspects of life that are thought of as personal choices in the United States.*

   theocratic   *adj.* *His brush with death gave him a theocratic certainty in the absolute rightness of his mission.*

   theocrat   *n.* an official of a theocracy, one who lives in a theocracy, or someone who espouses theocracy: *With the rise of the religious right, it began to look as if we would simply trade in the onerous bureaucrats for the potentially even more onerous theocrats.*

Religious Belief and Disbelief

Decisions of faith are personal, but once made, people often feel compelled to tell others about them. Fortunately, there are many ways of expressing what you believe—and whether you believe.

antinomianism   *n.* the belief of some Christians that salvation depends only on faith, independent of morality.

apostate   *n.* someone who has abandoned their religion or faith.
  apostate   *adj.* having to do with those who have abandoned their faith or religion
  apostasy   *n.* the abandonment of one's faith

henotheism   *n.* belief in or worship of a single god without denying the existence of others.

idolatry   *n.* the worship of statues or other representations of religious figures or gods, or worship of the gods in polytheistic religions.

kabala   *n.* a mystical Jewish system of beliefs which holds that the Scriptures are a coded text and that the universe came into being by radiating from God.

nihilism   *n.* rejection of religious beliefs.
  nihilist   *n.* one who rejects religion

quietist   *adj.* relating to a form of spiritual mysticism based on passive meditation.

sacralize   *v.* to make sacred or holy.

secularize *v.* to make something that is religious nonreligious or worldly.

theodicy *n.* vindication of the goodness and justness of the supreme being in allowing the existence of evil.

---

theodicy *n.* a vindication of the goodness and justness of the supreme being in allowing the existence of evil: *Why do bad things happen to good people? That would be one of the central questions for any theodicy to try to explain.*

thrall *n.* a state or condition of being bound by the influence of someone or something: *The school calendar remains in thrall to the needs of farming communities that are long gone.*

thrash/thresh see at S CONFUSABLES

throes *pl. n.* **1** a struggle: *The kids are in the throes of studying for exams.* ∗ *the throes of despair* **2** convulsions or serious pain: *Her brother collapsed in the throes of a severe asthma attack.*

thrones *n.* the seventh of nine orders of angels. See THE CELESTIAL HIERARCHY at **angel**.

timbre *n.* the quality of a sound that is particular to its source: *I could tell Frank was asleep in the living room; I recognized the timbre of his snore.*

timidity   *n.* cowardice; meekness: *Timidity has its advantages—you are less likely to be killed than are those who must fight to retain dominance, and learning coping strategies may help a species adapt to changing environments.* Antonym: **temerity**.

tinnient   *adj.* having a ringing sound: *Each time a train passes by I hear my grandmother's tinnient silver goblets shaking on their shelf.*

tinnitus   *n.* a continual ringing or whistling sound in the ear: *Tinnitus is a type of auditory phantom.* See also **tintinnabulation**.

tintinnabulation   *n.* a ringing sound, like the sound of bells: *In the distance you could hear the faint tintinnabulation of the wind chimes.* ∗ *On Wednesday evenings the bell-ringers at the nearby church practiced their tintinnabulation.* See also **tinnitus**.

tiro   *n.* See **tyro**

titanic   *adj.* of huge size or strength; enormous: *It took a titanic effort to finish the project on schedule.* ∗ *That tractor-trailer is titanic!*
    titanically *adv.* enormously: *The reaction was titanically out of proportion.*

tocsin   *n.* an alarm bell, or a warning of danger: *The president maintained he was not trying to sound the tocsin of war.*

tony *adj.* stylish; luxurious; pretentious: *We had dinner in the tony hotel restaurant.*

toponym *n.* **1** a place name: *Krakow's book traces the peachtree toponyms found in Atlanta to the English translation of the name for a Cherokee village, Pakanahuili.* **2** a word formed from a place name: *The toponym daiquiri is named for the Cuban town in which it purportedly, was first concocted.* Compare **eponym.**

torpid *adj.* sluggish, dull, or apathetic: *The high heat and humidity left the children torpid and uninterested in their usual games.*

tortuous/torturous see at T CONFUSABLES

tout *v.* **1** to solicit something, such as sales, business, bets, or votes: *They tout the T-shirts they silkscreen at flea markets.* **2** to recommend or promote: *Critics have been touting the film.*
    tout *n.* someone soliciting something, especially a person who sells tips on horse races: *The guy is a tout who hangs around the OTB place up the street.*

traduce *v.* to make false and malicious comments about someone or something; slander: *The plan was traduced and rejected out-of-hand by a panel whose animosity to anything but the status quo was all too clear.*

transfigure *v.* to change outwardly, usually for the better; to give a new and often spiritual look to something: *Metaphors transfigure us and reveal the meanings of our lives.*

    transfiguration *n.* change in appearance or quality, especially of a spiritual nature: *Looking at her now, we could see that her transfiguration was complete, that she was no longer the woman she had been.*

transgenic *adj.* relating to genetic material transferred from one species to another: *The hope is that the milk of these transgenic ewes will contain a substance that could one day be used to treat cystic fibrosis.* * *transgenic techniques*

transliterate *v.* to transcribe writing into the characters of a different alphabet or writing system: *He uses one system for rendering Russian speech, and another system for transliterating names.* * *Chinese is usually transliterated using the pinyin romanization system.*

    transliteration *n.* transcription into the characters of a different alphabet: *One cannot help being irritated by peculiarities in his method of transliteration.*

transpire see at T CONFUSABLES

treachery/treason see at T CONFUSABLES

trepidation *n.* fearful concern or alarm; apprehension: *Her decision to drive from Boston to Los Angeles caused her mother some trepidation.*

triforium *n., pl.* **triforia** a balcony space above the side aisle in the nave of a church: *We climbed up to the triforium where the balcony is given over to a small, stained glass museum.*

trig *adj.* fashionably fit; attractively trim: *The young woman serving as first mate was as trig and appealing as the boat, with appealing lines and exuding a feeling of vigor.*

troche *n.* a soothing lozenge or tablet containing medicine: *Dr. Tay prescribed a troche that made my throat happy but tasted like some sort of noxious weed.*

trochee *n.* a metrical foot in a poem which has one long syllable followed by a short one or one stressed syllable followed by an unstressed one

trompe l'oeil *n.* a painting style that creates the illusion of three-dimensional reality and that typically features statues, columns, or a view into a room: *The back wall of the small chapel was a trompe l'oeil of a choir balcony.*

troop see at T Confusables

trope *n.* a literary device such as irony or metaphor in which words are not used in their literal sense: *The high quality of writing in this article liberally sprinkled with tropes and allusions is not usual in the ordinary, run-of-the-mill gardening article.*

troupe see **troop/troupe** at T Confusables

trousseau *n., pl.* **trousseaux** the possessions a bride brings to her married life, especially clothing, linens, and household goods: *It took years for a frontier girl to ready a trousseau for the day she would marry.*

truant *adj.* not meeting one's responsibilities: *Novelists kill off their characters with such alacrity that it seems as if they feel they would be truant if they left them alive.*

truculent *adj.* **1** troublesome; quarrelsome: *We tackled the first section of code yesterday, but it's a truculent mess and could take several weeks to get straight.* **2** belligerent; hostile: *I'm sorry to say I had another run-in with that truculent young man who lives upstairs.* Synonyms: **bellicose**; **pugnacious**.

truncated *adj.* **1** having or seeming to have a part cut off: *I thought the truncated figures in the background left the painting looking incomplete.* **2** shortened or suddenly cut off: *The movie was a truncated adaptation of the novel that left too many loose ends.*

tumbrel, tumbril *n.* a farm cart that can be tipped up to empty it: *The manure-filled tumbrel was wheeled out of the barn.*

tumescent *adj.* **1** swelling: *A novel that describes the heroine's breathing as "gulping" and her breasts* *as "tumescent" is doomed.* ∗ *Tumescent joints could indicate Lyme disease.* **2** pretentious or overblown: *I can't bear listening to his boring, tumescent speech again.*

    tumescence *n.* a swelling or a swollen condition: *The tumescence and pain in her wrist had gotten worse.*

twee *adj.* overly cute; designed to be attractive in an artificially charming or syrupy way: *Victorian England loved those twee fairy paintings draped in gossamer and dripping with sentimentality.*

tyro, tiro *n.* a novice or beginner: *Downsizing leads to a workforce filled with tyros who have no experienced hands to lead them.*

U

CONFUSABLES

unartistic/inartistic   *Unartistic* means not inclined to produce art (*I can sing and dance,
but when it comes to painting, I'm pretty unartistic.*); *inartistic* means not considered to be
art (*inartistic doodles*), or not able to discern
art (*I know what I like, but I'm basically
inartistic.*).

unattached/detached   *Unattached* means not
married (*an unattached woman*), not seized in
legal proceedings (*His freelance income was
left unattached in the settlement.*), or not connected (*One boat was unattached and began
drifting away.*); *detached* means indifferent or
aloof (*a detached demeanor*), or can also mean
not connected (*a detached house*).

underlay/underlie   To *underlay* something
means to raise or support it by placing some-

thing under it (*Sand underlays the stones that make up the path.*); to *underlie* something is lend moral or theoretical support to it (*Fascist doctrine underlies their terrorist activities.*).

undulate/ripple *Undulate* means to move in smooth waves of any size (*Her hips undulated as she walked.*); *ripple* means to move in small waves (*The water rippled out from where the pebble landed.*).

uninterested/disinterested see **disinterested/ uninterested** at D CONFUSABLES

unravel/ravel see **ravel/unravel** at R CONFUS- ABLES

---

ubiquitous *adj.* always present or in evidence: *Beggars are ubiquitous on the streets of the capital.* **ubiquity** *n.* the state of existing everywhere at the same time: *The ubiquity of violence against the poor is an alarming fact of life.*

ukase *n.* an order or ruling, especially one that is unfair or arbitrary: *With only the slightest hint of reluctance, she carried out my mother's ukases.*

ululation *n.* a howl, hoot, or wail: *The children were frightened by the ululations of the wind.*

unartistic see at U CONFUSABLES

unattached see at U CONFUSABLES

underlay/underlie see at U CONFUSABLES

undulate   *v.* to move with a wavelike motion, or to form a wavelike shape: *We tried to spot our nieces Cory and Bridget in the undulating line of marchers coming down the avenue.* See at U CONFUSABLES.

unedifying   *adj.* uninformative and not enlightening: *The Clinton impeachment proceedings offered the unedifying spectacle of lawyer attacking lawyer.*

unequivocal   *adj.* clear and unambiguous; unqualified: *The president's denial was not unequivocal.*
   unequivocally   *adj. He unequivocally denied any responsibility.*

uninterested see **disinterested/uninterested** at D CONFUSABLES

unravel see **ravel/unravel** at R CONFUSABLES

usurp   *v.* to wrongfully or illegally take or use something: *The company had usurped the material for use on a CD—a use not covered by the original contract.* * *An attempt to throw the election and usurp the committee's authority was stopped.*
   usurpation   *n. The mayor's appointment of a committee to change the city charter at this time is seen by some as usurpation.*

utopian   *adj.* **1** perfect; ideal; relating to unrealistic plans of perfection; idealistic: *The company was founded by a utopian dreamer whose policies made it a pleasant, comfortable workplace for some, frustrating for others.* ∗ *utopian reformers* **2** pertaining to a utopia, an ideal society: *a nineteenth-century utopian community*

utopia   *n.* an ideal state or society where all social, political, and moral aspects of life have been perfected, or a fictional story about such a place Antonyms: **dystopian, dystopia**.

In the fictional work *Utopia* written by Sir Thomas More, Utopia is an island nation with ideal social and political systems.

V

CONFUSABLES

venial/venal *Venial* means forgivable, and is usually applied to sins (*Her white lies were venial sins.*); *venal* means corruptible (*The city was overrun with venal politicians.*).

venturesome/venturous/adventuresome/ adventurous see **adventurous/adventuresome/ venturous/venturesome** at A CONFUSABLES

viable/possible *Viable* means capable of continued life or existence (*The fetus is viable from about seven months.*); *possible* means having the potential to be achieved (*a possible solution*).

vulgar/obscene/profane see **obscene/profane/ vulgar** at O CONFUSABLES

vacuity *n.* emptiness, or a lack of ideas, intelligence, or awareness: *the vacuity of the gray-blue ocean* * *The intellectual vacuity of some of the proposals was dismaying.*

    vacuous *adj.* *She sent a vacuous response to my memo, so I guess I'd better go talk to her.* * *a vacuous stare*

vacuous *adj.* See at **vacuity**.

vade mecum *n., pl.* **vade mecums** something a person often carries with them, such as a small reference or guidebook: *The man next to me had out those twin vade mecums of the late 90s commuter, a cell phone and an electronic organizer.*

vagary *n.* an unpredictable activity, action, event, or occurrence: *A single ill-conceived decision can turn life on its head, bringing consequences that are the result of vagary and destroying any carefully made plans.*

valediction *n.* something done or said as a farewell or to mark a leave-taking: *We'd lived two years in Cambridge and felt some sort of valediction was in order when the time came to return home.*

    valedictory *adj.* *Valedictory remarks can be trite and clichéd.*

valetudinarian *n.* a sickly person; an invalid: *We visit every day to gossip, and try to find things to interest her, but nothing pleases this grouchy valetudinarian.*

vanquish   *v.* to defeat, overcome, or conquer: *That wonderful meal vanquished both my hunger and my bad mood. * The mayor vanquished his opponents in the gubernatorial primary.*

vapid   *adj.* lacking interest, dull, flat, or boring: *If I spent all day writing vapid advertising copy, I'd be out of a job—my ads are catchy. * I need something different to read—this vapid prose is putting me to sleep.*
   vapidity   *n. The vapidity of some of the pieces people send us to consider for publication is amazing.*

variegated   *adj.* diverse, varied, or having a variety of colors: *Birdhouses in variegated colors had been placed on top of the brick wall.*

vassal   *n.* a servant, subordinate, or follower: *Our North American neighbors would reject the notion that they are vassals of the United States.*

vatic, vatical   *adj.* like a prophet: *Passersby were drawn by the street preacher's vatic exhortations.*

vaunted   *adj.* praised highly, or boasted of: *The program tested the company's vaunted project-management skills.*

velleity   *n.* an inclination or wish for something with no action taken to achieve it, the weakest form of volition: *She seems to never really want anything,* *and if she says she does, her want is a small thing, mere velleity—the shallowest of desires.* See **volition**.

venal *adj.* corrupt; able to be bribed or bought or compromised: *Robin took up with New York's S& M subculture, as venal and self-absorbed a group as exists in that famously self-absorbed city.* See **venial/ venal** at V CONFUSABLES.

venial *adj.* minor or forgivable: *No one would make a fuss over so venial an error.* * *venial sin* See at V CONFUSABLES. Antonym: **mortal**.

venturesome/venturous see **adventurous/adventure- some/venturous/venturesome** at A CONFUSABLES

veracity *n.* accuracy; habitual truthfulness and honesty: *The strongest indication of his veracity is the candor with which he acknowledges his capacity for failure.*

verbalism *n.* **1** a word, or the phrasing or wording of something: *Your verbalism makes it abundantly difficult to wrest any meaning from your text.* **2** a wordy phrase or expression that lacks substantial meaning: *Crimes against women need to be ad- dressed with effective action, not mere verbalism.*

verisimilitude *n.* the appearance of truth; likeli- hood or probability: *They manufacture knicknacks that people take to have a certain historical verisimil- itude, although no such object existed at the time.*

verity   *n.* something real or true; truth: *The narratives of holy books often deal with ethical verities.*

vernacular   *n.* **1** the architectural style common to a particular region, period, or culture: *Housing redevelopment near the city center is in the vernacular, blending with existing stock.* **2** the native language of a place or as spoken by a particular group, or the particular vocabulary of a group of people: *French is used in the schools, but the vernacular is used at home.*
   vernacular   *adj.* **1** relating to the architectural style common to a particular region, period, or culture: *vernacular design* **2** relating to the spoken language or vocabulary of a particular group of people: *The slam last night showcased vernacular poetry.* * *the military vernacular*

vernal   *adj.* having to do with springtime: *The vernal landscape blossomed.* * *the vernal equinox*

verso   *n.* the page of a manuscript meant to be read second, or a left-hand page in a book Compare **recto.**

vertiginous   *adj.* causing a spinning, tilting, or dizzying sensation: *The stones stand at varying angles, creating a vertiginous effect.*

vestigial   *adj.* relating to evidence of something that no longer exists: *The appendix is a vestigial part of the gut that was important in animals whose diets were composed of more fiber than humans consume.*

vexation *n.* an annoyance, a cause of annoyance, or the state of being annoyed: *There comes a point where you can't brush off these vexations and stay cheerful.* * *Richie's vexation was caused more by the heavy traffic then by anything you said.*

vexatious *adj.* troublesome and annoying: *As we dig deeper into what really happened, some interesting yet vexatious issues rise to the surface.*

viable see at V CONFUSABLES

viaticum *n.*, *pl.* **viaticums**, **viatica** the money or things needed for a journey: *With new boots, full packs, a set of maps, and a small viaticum, they set out to hike the Appalachian Trail for their honeymoon trip.*

vicarious *adj.* **1** substituting for or taking the place of something or someone else: *A replica of a colonial village can help us understand life at that time, but a vicarious simulation will never tell the full story.* **2** shared by imagining the experience of someone else: *When my sister won the election, I felt a vicarious thrill.*

vicissitudes *pl.*, *n.* changing conditions: *She took a philosophical attitude about the vicissitudes of fortune and fate.*

violaceous *adj.* having a bluish purple color: *She'd been in the water too long—her lips were violaceous and the skin of her fingers wrinkled.*

virago *n.* a loud, bad-tempered woman; a shrew: *They claimed she was a shameless hussy, a virago who could be counted on for nothing but trouble.* Synonym: **termagant**.

virgule *n.* a slash mark (/) used in writing to separate alternatives, such as *either/or*, to represent the word *per,* as in *miles/hour*, or to show where lines of verse end when they are printed continuously, as in *Ride a cockhorse / to Banbury Cross*

viridian, **veridian** *n.* a blue-green color: *I was delighted with the lovely veridian he'd painted the entrance hall in.*

virtues *n.* the fifth of nine orders of angels. See THE CELESTIAL HIERARCHY at **angel**.

visceral *adj.* instinctive; felt internally: *The alarm I felt was visceral and quickly turned to anger.*

viscid *adj.* thick, sticky, and gooey, or coated with something like this: *She slathered her sunburn with a viscid layer of aloe.*

vitiate *v.* to cause something to be impaired or less effective: *The project was vitiated by revisions that wouldn't have been needed if everyone had been consulted at the start.*

vitriol *n.* speech or feelings that are caustic and abrasive: *Article after article dumped vitriol on those* *who, in retrospect, were foolish enough to embrace the radical left in the 30s, 40s, and 50s.*

    vitriolic *adj.* *His vitriolic attacks on those who have the temerity to disagree with him make me think he does not understand the meaning of the term "public servant."*

vituperative *adj.* verbally abusive or censorious: *He can turn in an instant from being charming and polite to being aggressive and vituperative.*

vivacious *adj.* lively and animated in speech and expression: *The new sales director has a wonderfully vivacious personality.* ∗ *Thirty-four vivacious teens came pouring off the bus.*
    vivaciousness *n.* *I think we need someone with more vivaciousness to make the on-site presentations.*
    Synonyms: **effervescent; effervescence**.

vivarium *adj.* a place where the natural environment of particular plants and animals is simulated: *Much planning went into creating the museum's tropical butterfly vivarium.*

vociferous *adj.* loud and insistent, in a way that demands attention: *I thought the proposal was pretty innocuous, but public reaction to it was so vociferous that I realized it must be a pretty powerful idea.*

volition *n.* the act of choosing or a choice made by one's own will: *She is doing this of her own volition.* ∗ *an act of volition.* Compare **velleity**.

volitional *adj. Martin's intrusion on our conversation was clearly volitional.*

voracious   *adj.* **1** wanting or eating large amounts of food: *He was voracious, consuming everything put before him.* **2** having a great desire or eagerness for something; greedy: *Tyler's voracious appetite for books is unquenchable.* * *a voracious pursuit of knowledge.* Compare **ravenous**. See also **rapacious**.

votive   *adj.* devotional, or undertaken to fulfill a promise: *At a certain votive stage in my relationship with cartoons, I cut out favorite comic strips and made little books of them.*

vulgar see **obscene/profane/vulgar** at O CONFUS-ABLES

W

CONFUSABLES

warp/woof *Warp* is the number of threads strung lengthwise on a loom; *woof* is yarn threaded between the warp.

winsome/winning A *winsome* person has a pleasingly childlike innocence (*a winsome young man who still loves games and sports*); a *winning* aspect of someone's personality is a pleasing aspect (*a winning smile*).

woolen/woolly *Woolen* means made of wool (*a woolen scarf*); *woolly* means covered with wool (*a woolly sheep*), fuzzy in thought or speech (*After a couple of martinis, the mind can get pretty woolly.*), or made of wool.

wrack/rack see **rack/wrack** at R CONFUSABLES

warp see at W CONFUSABLES

wary *adj.* cautious and on one's guard: *Bob's run-in with the police didn't seem to make him any warier.* * *She gave him a wary look.* Synonym: **chary**.

watershed *n.* an important point or transition: *It was hoped that the cease-fire would prove a watershed and a treaty would soon follow.*

   watershed *adj. Acquisition of the new subsidiary was not seen as a watershed event for either party.*

wax *v.* to grow gradually, as in size, strength, or extent: *He began to wax enthusiastic.* * *the waxing moon*

welkin *n.* **1** the heavens, or the firmament above the sky: *His voice bellows out against the welkin, raging against the injustice that is his life.* **2** the upper atmosphere: *The Concorde climbed to the welkin, where the darkness of space could be glimpsed.*

wether *n.* a castrated male sheep or goat

whorl *n.* a spiral, coil, or swirl, or something that suggests such a shape: *The illustrations had more whorls and whirligigs than you could shake a stick at.*

wimple *n.* a piece of clothing that covers the neck, cheeks, and chin, leaving only the face visible, now rarely worn except by some nuns: *She wore the* *traditional habit with long black veil and white wimple, a crucifix swinging from her waist.*

winsome/winning see at W CONFUSABLES

woof see **warp/woof** at W CONFUSABLES

woolen/woolly see at W CONFUSABLES

wrack see **rack/wrack** at R CONFUSABLES

Words for Words

It was probably not very long after our cave-dwelling ancestors first developed language to describe the world around them that they developed the need to start describing the words they were using to describe the world. Although clearly predating postmodernism, this field of self-reference is a goldmine of verbalism.

alliterate   *v.* to repeat a sound in two or more words in a group, such as the same first or last letters of several words in a line of poetry, as *lilac lilies line the lane.*
   alliterating   *adj.*

anagram   *n.* a word or phrase made from the reordered letters of another word or phrase, as *stain* made from *satin.*

aphaeresis, apheresis *n.* the loss of letters or sounds at the beginnings of a word, resulting in a new, shorter word, as *round* made from *around*.

aphorism *n.* a wise or clever saying.

apothegm, apophthegm *n.* a short, clever saying that instructs.

assonance *n.* resemblance or similarity of vowel sounds, or the repetition of identical or similar vowel sounds with changes in the consonants.

chiasmus *n.* a reversal of the order of words in two phrases that are otherwise identical or parallel, as *It's better to be looked over than to be overlooked*.

cognate *adj.* related in origin to other words in related languages that have developed from the same root.
    cognate *n.* a word in one language that is related to one in another language.

colloquial *adj.* conversational, or appropriate to everyday speech and writing.

contumely *n.* mean, harsh, or cruel language. that displays contempt or feelings of superiority toward others.

contumelious *adj.* of language, mean, harsh, or cruel

creole *n.* a native language that originated in the combining of two or more distinct other languages.

decline *v.* to inflect a word, or to recite the inflected forms of a word.
    declension *n.* the inflected forms of a word considered as a group, or the recitation of the inflected forms of a word

emendation *n.* a correction or change, usually to a text.

eponym *n.* the person from whom something takes its name.
    eponymous, eponymic *adj.* named for, or thought to have been named for, a particular person
    eponymously *adv.*

etymon *n.* **1** an earlier form of a word in the same language or in a language from which it developed **2** a word or part of a word from which compounds and derivatives are formed **3** a foreign word from which a given loan word is derived.

exegesis *n.* an explanation, critical analysis, or interpretation, usually of a text.

exegete, exegetist   *n.* a textual analysis
exegetic, exegetical   *adj.* explanatory or critical of a text.

heteronym   *n.* one of two or more words that have identical spellings but different meanings and pronunciations, such as *lead* (a metal) and *lead* (to direct or guide).

lemma   *n., pl.* **lemmas** or **lemmata** a word or phrase as it appears in a glossary.

logogram, logograph, ideogram   *n.* a written symbol or sign that represents a word.

onomatopoeia   *n.* the creation or use of a word that imitates the sound associated with the thing or action it refers to, as *buzz*.

palindrome   *n.* a word, phrase, sentence, or number that reads the same backward or forward, as *Anna*.
   palindromic   *adj.*

patois   *n.* a regional variation of a language that differs from the language's standard form; a dialect.

perorate   *v.* to make a long, grandiloquent speech.
   peroration   *n.*

petroglyph   *n.* writing or a picture carved into a rock

pidgin *n.* a language combining elements of two or more languages that developed as a form of communication between peoples who speak different native languages and that has a less formal and developed structure and grammar than a creole.

prosaic *adj.* relating to prose rather than poetry.

rhapsodic *adj.* expressed with passion and enthusiasm.

rhetoric *n.* **1** the art or skill of writing or speaking effectively **2** a type of language suitable for a particular audience.
   rhetorical *adj.* said only for effect
   rhetorically *adv.*

semiotics *n.* a theory of signs and symbols used in language.
   semiotician *n.* one who can successfully use signs and symbols in language, or one who studies their use

sobriquet *n.* a nickname.

synecdoche *n.* a figure of speech in which the word for an individual, part, or substance is used instead of the word for a group, whole, or manufactured thing, or the word for the group, etc., is used for the individual, etc., as *teachers* instead of *Ms. McCurdy*.

trope   *n.* a literary device such as irony or metaphor in which words are not used in their literal sense.

verbalism   *n.* **1** a word, or the phrasing or wording of something **2** a wordy phrase or expression that lacks substantial meaning.

vernacular   *n.* the native language of a place or as spoken by a particular group, or the particular vocabulary of a group of people.
    vernacular   *adj.* relating to the spoken language or vocabulary of a particular group of people.

vitriol   *n.* caustic, abrasive speech.
    vitriolic   *adj.*

zeugma   *n.* the use of a word in two different meanings to modify or act on two different words in a single sentence, as *lost* in *She lost her car keys and her patience.*

X, Y & Z

yea/yeah   *Yea* means yes, and is used when voting orally (*Cast your vote by saying yea or nay.*); it can also mean hurrah (*Yea! Our team won!*), or to an indicated extent (*I caught a fish that was yea big.*); *yeah* means yes, and is used in conversation and informal writing (*"Would you like more pie?" "Yeah, I wouldn't mind another piece."*).

Zeitgeist   *n.* characteristic of a particular time and place: *Say what you will about his politics and his style, he has a grasp of the Zeitgeist that makes him unassailable in the popular media.*

zeugma   *n.* the use of a word in two different meanings to modify or act on two different words in a single sentence: *The use of "lost" is a zeugma in the sentence, "She lost her wallet and her mind at the market."*